This Book Belongs To:

_____

_____

ROBIN HOOD

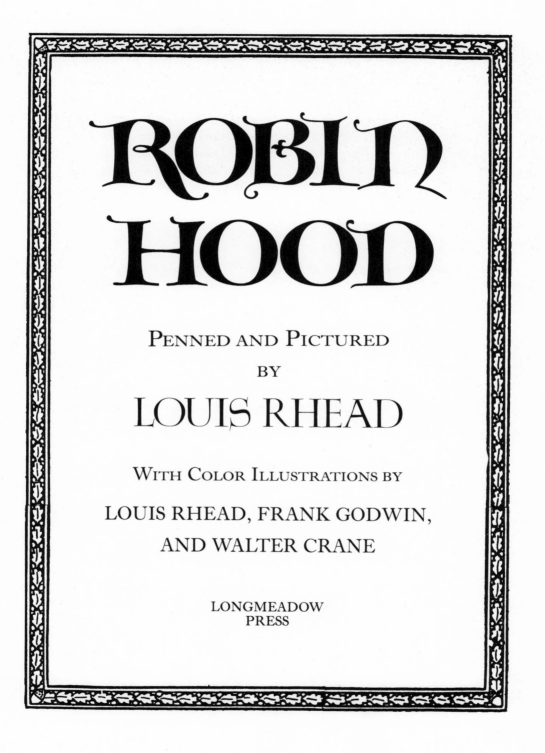

ROBIN HOOD

Penned and Pictured

by

LOUIS RHEAD

With Color Illustrations by

LOUIS RHEAD, FRANK GODWIN,
AND WALTER CRANE

LONGMEADOW
PRESS

This book is printed on acid-free paper. It surpasses the standards set for Permanence of Paper for Printed Library Materials.

Originally published under the title *Bold Robin Hood and His Outlaw Band.*

"Preface to this Illustrated Edition," Foreword, and compilation copyright © 1988 by dilithium Press, Ltd., Children's Classics Division. All rights reserved.

This 1991 edition is published exclusively by Longmeadow Press, 201 High Ridge Road, P.O. 10218, Stamford, CT 06904, by arrangement with Outlet Book Company, Inc., a Random House Company, 225 Park Avenue South, New York, New York 10003.

Printed and Bound in the United States of America

Cover design by Clair Moritz

ISBN 0-681-41162-7

10 9 8 7 6 5 4 3 2 1

A TABLE OF THE CONTENTS

LIST OF COLOR ILLUSTRATIONS

PREFACE TO THIS ILLUSTRATED EDITION

THREE outstanding artists display their powerful talents in bringing to life the myth and romance of *Robin Hood* in this special Children's Classics edition, the latest in the series of stories illustrated by distinguished artists of the past century.

Louis Rhead, an Englishman who worked at the turn of the century, both "penned and pictured" the exploits of this extraordinary hero and his gallant band of outlaws in Sherwood Forest. The text and the black-and-white illustrations are thus beautifully integrated, the product of Rhead's sparkling vision of a man he sees as "the most humane and princely of outlaws" and his band of "merry fellows without guile, bold and fair in fight . . . striking hard at tyranny and cruelty." He has given us full-scale portraits of many of the characters with keen insight and wit, adventure scenes with action and humor, elegant decorations and richly detailed vignettes that ornament the pages, and has provided the striking full-color tableau of Robin and Little John struggling on a bridge.

Frank Godwin, an American artist who worked in the first part of this century, contributed four of the color plates in this edition. Little is written or known about him today, but his brilliant and sensual renderings are remarkable and should have assured him lasting recognition.

Finally, Walter Crane, the renowned nineteenth-century artist and designer, created three of the fine color illustrations seen here.

It is not surprising that three such diverse artists should have been drawn to this subject. Throughout the centuries, the Robin Hood legend has had innumerable interpreters and portrayals, because Robin Hood's persona has ignited men's imaginations. Each artist and each writer contributes something new, something of himself, to the tradition, and if their contributions are not always identical—as indeed, they may not always be, here—still they are exciting and richly satisfying to readers, who will be the happy beneficiaries of this heritage.

CLAIRE BOOSS
Series Editor

1988

FOREWORD

MANY attempts have been made to establish the authenticity of Robin Hood, the benevolent outlaw whose daring exploits leave us breathless while we inwardly cheer him on. But certainly more important than Robin Hood's origin is his permanent position in our lore, for Robin Hood has fired our imaginations and become as real to us as any flesh-and-blood historical figure.

The first allusion to Robin Hood appears in William Langland's *Piers Plowman* (circa 1378) when one character, Sloth, professes his knowledge of the rhymes of Robin Hood. This reference suggests, of course, that Robin had already been established as a popular figure in the ballads of the day. The *Lyttel Geste of Robyn Hode*, also dating from the fourteenth century, contains many of the adventures familiar today, and marks the first appearance of the scheming Sheriff of Nottingham, whose rivalry with the famous outlaw remains the best known of all Robin Hood lore.

Surprisingly, the activity most often ascribed to Robin and his merry men—robbing the rich and giving to the poor—was not a prevalent theme in the early ballads. Robin Hood's true love, Maid Marian, was also a later addition to the legend, and it has been suggested that she was borrowed from an unrelated French pastoral play, *Jeu de Robin et Marion*. While much of the material for Robin Hood's adventures dates from medieval times, authors throughout the ages have seen fit to embellish these tales and shade Robin's character in accordance with their own personal visions. It is quite possible to find Robin Hood portrayed as either yeoman or nobleman, thief or rebel, hero or buffoon. He is usually found engaging in combat or engineering complicated plots requiring artifice or disguise. Typically, he is cast as an agent of retribution, a constant vexation to corrupt government and church officials.

In this edition of *Robin Hood,* Louis Rhead, working during the early part of this century, limned in word and picture a Robin Hood of many facets. Though born a nobleman, the son of the Earl of Huntingdon, Robin feels closely akin to the peasants who surround him in childhood. From them he learned "...to give and take hard knocks, to be plain and downright in speech, to value every man at his true worth, to despise a coward and to love a brave, honest fellow even if he were of low degree." In short, "despite his noble birth he was a yeoman at heart."

The rash, heedless manner in which Robin enters into spirited combat with stalwart strangers, and the invariable bumps and bruises he receives make him often a comic figure. During his first encounter with Friar Tuck and his imposing mastiffs, for instance, we find Robin scurrying up the limbs of the nearest tree. Even a disguised Maid Marian, not recognizing her beloved, gets the better of him in brief swordplay. Yet in spite of these blows to his image of invincibleness, Robin Hood remains a man to be admired. He is at all times willing to fight his own battles and to accept the consequences of his actions. For this reason, he is a hero in the eyes of the men of Sherwood who follow him.

Robin also enjoys relieving worldly priests and greedy government leaders of their fat purses, but his thieving seems a justifiable punishment for the hypocrisy his victims exhibit. In the hands of Rhead, Robin Hood becomes a complex character who not only inspires awe because of his lively escapades, but who also commands respect for his steadfast adherence to principle; while embodying heroic qualities he remains a man with flaws and imperfections that endear him to us.

Rhead's perception of the outlaw band and his style of storytelling outshine many other versions of the tale. Many collections emphasize Robin's thirst for revenge; the band's penchant for murdering their oppressors; and Robin's superhuman, almost mystical, powers. In contrast, Rhead's portrait is a much more chivalrous and humanized one. Robin and several of his men are seen as victims of chance or of the improper administration of the law. The young Will Gamwell is banished when he kills an assassin involved in a plot by relatives to inherit his estate. Robin himself ponders "...that an outlaw's life had not been his choice, but it had been forced upon him, willy-nilly."

In spite of their misfortunes, the men of Sherwood are, for the most part, devoid of murderous intentions. Instead, they relish devising elaborate ruses and donning cunning disguises to rid their enemies of both their excessive wealth and their extreme vanity. Robin, disguised as a merchant who sells his wares at cheap prices, is able, on more than one occasion, to lure the bargain-hunting Sheriff of Nottingham deep into Sherwood Forest before the outlaw reveals his identity. Inevitably, the embarrassed sheriff is made to eat humble pie—as he is compelled to partake of a sumptuous feast prepared by the merry band. Robin and his men are, first and foremost, clever pranksters, and their ploys often save innocents from the gallows; young women from loveless, arranged marriages; and honest citizens from poverty.

When battles to the death do occur in Rhead's Sherwood, they are followed by remorse or introspection. After killing a forester in self-defense when he was a young lad of fifteen, Robin recognizes the gravity of his action. We are told, "He knew that men slew and were slain in fair fight, but the thought that he had taken a life was very bitter to him." When Robin is an older man, his less trustworthy followers hang the sheriff in a fit of rage. It is this foul deed which brings about the death of Robin Hood—for, from that moment, his spirit is broken and his will to live fails him. When the creed to which Robin and his men swore allegiance is violated, Robin, in essence, chooses to shorten his life in an attempt to justify his many years as champion of the common man.

Louis Rhead's stirring accounts of archery contests, quarter-staff fights, and daring rescues are complemented by lush descriptions of the idyllic landscape of Sherwood Forest. Rhead's elegant, lucid, and evocative prose brings to the text the flavor of days long past while still remaining accessible to the young reader. Found along this journey through Nottingham and Sherwood are unforgettable characters with such names as Allan-a-Dale, Sir Richard O' the Lea, Sir Guy of Gisbourne, and Dick O' Branbury who will not only surprise, delight, and alarm, but also teach us that heroism is no more than charitableness to a fellow human being. The men of Sherwood have found in their chronicler, Louis Rhead, a talented marksman who carefully aims, and pierces our hearts with this moving testament to the unwavering generosity and honesty of their leader, Robin Hood.

LEE SANTINI
Editor

New York
1988

EDITORIAL NOTE
The modern reader may be surprised to discover old-fashioned styles of punctuation and spelling, but these have been retained in order to convey the flavor of the original work.

RICHARD CŒUR DE LION

IN this version of the Robin Hood tradition I have endeavored
to group the various incidents in logical progression, and to
connect them as intimately as possible with the customs and
manners of the age in which it is supposed he lived—the latter
part of the twelfth century. Moreover, I have made character-
portraits of all the principals in the legend, paying particular
attention to historical accuracy in the matter of dress, arms, and
other accessories. It is a singular circumstance that the name
of an outlawed individual of the twelfth century should remain
as well known as that of Richard the Lion-hearted or the Black
Prince; that the echoes of his personality should be preserved
in household ballad and fireside tale; that his words and deeds
continue to be a familiar part of the Anglo-Saxon heritage—
all this is pretty conclusive proof that Robin Hood was an actual
living personage. There is nothing mythical about the achieve-
ments of the renowned outlaw; and though medieval English
historians never mentioned this notable man, it was probably
his avowed enmity to churchmen that caused the monks to refrain
from rendering homage to his virtues. History, in former times,
was written by none but monks.

It is remarkable that one of the best stories of Robin Hood
was written and illustrated by an American artist who had never
set foot on English soil. In this latter respect I am more for-
tunate, having been born in the same country as Robin Hood
and having passed much of my early life in roaming about what
still remains of Sherwood and Needwood forests. I have endeavored to retain the quaint, simple, yet direct style of the
ballads, which are surprisingly unaffected and natural in their

AUTHOR'S PREFACE

appeal to the youthful mind. These ballads supply the material for all but three of the twenty-five chapters, and the titles are printed on the contents-page. The first three chapters are original matter, because no ballad describes and history is silent concerning the childhood and youth of Robin Hood. Most of the earlier versions begin with Robin at his meeting with Little John, when he was a full-fledged outlaw of middle age. Some of the ballads are very ancient—one, in particular, was printed in black letter by Wynken de Worde about 1489, and is now preserved in the public library at Cambridge. Others are of later date, belonging to the time of Henry the Eighth, and none are later than the period of Charles the Second.

The map of Royal hunting forests is intended to show only those places which are connected with Robin Hood's life, omitting the New Forest and other local stretches of woodland lying in the south of England. It is stated that England at this period was so covered with woods that a squirrel could hop from tree to tree across the entire country. The great Watling Street and Ermine Street roads, built by the Romans eight hundred years before, were still in fair condition in the time of Robin Hood. This map will doubtless be of greater service to American boys than to their English cousins, for no English boy is ignorant of the where-abouts of Sherwood and Nottingham.

Finally, I have derived Robin Hood's character and personality from the testimony of the old balladists and strolling minstrels who composed their rimes to be sung to their harps, and who pictured him as the most humane and princely of outlaws. Robin Hood and his merry men were not ordinary cutthroats, but a band of merry fellows without guile, bold and fair in fight, courteous and kind to women and children, bountiful to the poor and needy, and striking hard at cruelty and tyranny in a period when there were few to take the part of the poor and unlettered man. My Robin Hood will be found a brave, virtuous, and tactful leader, who wisely tested in personal combat each new recruit before he was allowed to join the band, and who was loved and revered by all for his many excellent and amiable qualities.

GREAT SEAL of HENRY II. AND RICHARD COEUR de LEON

A MAP TO SHOW THE SITUATION of ROYAL HUNTING
FORESTS WHERE ROBIN HOOD LIVED, A·D 1160~1247

STRATHCLYDE

PLOMPTON
FOREST

THREVESDALE
FOREST

YORK

DUBLIN

IRISH SEA

MANCHESTER

SHERWOOD
FOREST

CHESTER

LINCOLN

NOTTINGHAM

IRELAND

DERBY

NORTH
SEA

WREXHAM

SHERWOOD
FOREST

STAFFORD

WALES

WARWICK

WATLING STREET

R. SEVERN

R. AVON

LONDON

R. THAMES

CANTERBURY

DOVER

CALAIS

EXETER

FLANDERS

ENGLISH CHANNEL

NORMANDY

ROUEN

R. SEINE

BRITTANY

I

ROBIN HOOD—HIS BIRTH AND BOYHOOD

The Earl of Huntingdon, nobly born,
   That came of noble blood,
To Marion went, with good intent,
   By the name of Robin Hood.

IN the reign of King Henry II., there lived on an estate near Locksley Village in England, about two miles from the famous old town of Uttoxeter in the county of Stafford and almost on the borders of the Royal Forest of Needwood, a nobleman named William Fitzooth, Earl of Huntingdon. Earl William was a valliant warrior, and, a man of honorable fame. Like so many of the knights and nobles in that troubled age, he spent most of his time away from home, fighting in the great wars and petty quarrels that were always afoot in England or France, in Normandy, Ireland, or Wales. But during the brief intervals of peace he would return to take his ease in his strong castle, and at such times it was his chief delight to train and teach his sturdy young son, Robert.

When the boy was but five years old his father would lift him up to ride before him upon the great black war-steed through the

ROBIN HOOD

winding fern-clad paths of Needwood Forest. Next to fighting, the Earl loved hunting—whether with hawk or hound, with bow or boar-spear—and he always took Robert with him when he rode forth into the forest with his woodsmen and his dogs. Often the boy would shout with glee when he saw his father pierce with his spear and pin to earth a savage wild boar which the great dogs had driven right into their path. Again, gazing down a leafy glade with his sharp blue eyes, he would see a great hart come leaping, affrighted by the baying hounds. Then his father, who had been waiting with tense muscles and steady nerves, would raise his mighty bow of yew and draw the arrow clear to its head, the feathers brushing his cheek. The next instant, with a low hum, the cloth-yard shaft would be loosed, and the stag, smitten through the shoulder, would rise on its haunches and fall to its knees in death. Ever and anon Robert would shoot with his own little bow at the squirrels chattering and playing among the leafy branches. He was a good marksman even then, and it gladdened his father's heart to see him bring down many a squirrel, martin, or sable.

In those far-off days there was no attending school. The children of the rich barons were trained from their earliest years in war-like exercises and in the rules of chivalry. They were taught to be brave and honorable and courteous, to ride and to fight. Robert grew apace into a tall youth, well skilled in the use of arms. Yet he knew little of the great world. He bore himself as befitted an earl's son, with gentleness and yet with authority, but he had been reared almost in the forest, among yeomen and peasants. Of them he learned many good lessons— to give and take hard knocks, to be plain and downright in speech, to value every man at his true worth, to despise a coward and to love a brave, honest fellow, even if he were of low degree. Despite his noble birth he was a yeoman at heart.

Up to his twelfth year he enjoyed a merry, care-free life, saddened only by his father's long absences. Boy as he was, he practised with broadsword and quarter-staff, for in those days a man who had not learned to defend himself in his youth would

ROBERT WOULD SHOOT WITH HIS OWN LITTLE BOW
AT THE SQUIRRELS

ROBIN HOOD

have been in a sorry plight. But of all weapons he loved the long-bow best. He fashioned his own bows and arrows and used them constantly, so that ere long none had a steadier hand nor a truer eye. In knowledge of woodcraft he became the equal of the old foresters. He had a nimble wit, loved good company and manly sports. He was always present at the fairs and merry-making in Locksley and the near-by villages when the sturdy yeomen wrestled or fought with quarter-staves for prizes—a ram, a bull, a real gold ring, or a pipe of wine. But he was never so happy as when treading the soft, loamy, flower-bedecked sward of Needwood Forest that stretched for miles and miles, thickly covered with beech, oak, and chestnut trees.

When Robert was twelve years old news came of his father's death. Earl William had joined the army with which King Henry was invading Ireland. Landing at Waterford, the King marched toward Dublin to fight a famous native prince named Strongbow, and at the storming of one of the enemies' castles Earl William was struck down headlong from his horse by a barbed and poisoned arrow which pierced his eye through a crevice in his helmet. Thus Robert became an orphan, for his mother had died the previous year.

It was at about this time that Thomas a Becket, Archbishop of Canterbury, was foully murdered. King Henry had reached the age of forty, and had four sons living: Henry, in his eighteenth year; Richard, in his fifteenth; Geoffrey, in his fourteenth; and John, in his sixth. These were the sons of the good Queen Eleanor.

Robert wept grievously when he heard that his father was dead, and for many days he moped and felt bitterly toward the whole world. But at length he took courage, telling himself that from now on he must play the man. As time passed, his grief became less sharp; but there was a budding fear in his heart lest his uncle, now his guardian, might not prove true to his trust. This fear proved all too well advised, for his uncle was a reckless spend-thrift, insomuch that by the time the boy was fifteen his castle and broad lands, his serfs and cattle, were all forfeited. So

ROBIN HOOD

Robert's guardian, to escape the trouble in store for him, wended his way to the wars, leaving his poor young nephew to follow in the same path—or perchance to seek an asylum in the forests of his own and the neighboring counties of Nottingham, Derby, and York.

II

WHY ROBERT FITZOOTH CHANGED HIS NAME

There are twelve months in all the year,
  As I hear many say;
But the merriest month in all the year
  Is the merry month of May.

ON a bright May morn in the year of our Lord 1175 a youth strode with a rapid gait along the woodland path on the very edge of Need-wood Forest. Though it was yet early in the day, the sun was high and warm; the throstle and blackbird sang; the cuckoo from a high tree-top called the double note to his mate, and all the woods seemed glad. The bright yellow-green buds were just bursting forth, and the forest sward as far as eye could reach was a huge carpet of bright azure bluebells that gave a rich odor to the fresh morning air. The tall, comely lad, straight as a young birch, was scarce fifteen winters old, yet it needed but a glance to see that he was a proper youth, stout and bold. He had the keen bright eyes of a falcon, full, rounded lips, and a complexion deeply tanned His auburn curls hung down from beneath a jaunty cap of buckskin dyed old-gold, on the side of which, pointing upward, was buckled the middle tail-feather of a cock pheasant. He wore a deep olive-green jerkin, or coat, and the hose on his well-formed limbs fitted like a glove. His tough

[7]

ROBIN HOOD

yew long-bow hung from his shoulder in such a manner as to be instantly ready when needed. His beautifully embroidered quiver, chock-full of cloth-yard arrows, was slung from his shoulder-belt on the left side. From the red girdle drawn tightly round his waist hung a sheathed dagger or hunting-knife, and below it, fastened by straps, was a leathern pouch containing all his worldly possessions—his mother's rosary and gold ring, as well as food for the day, some sliced brawn and wheaten cakes. He had already gone many miles from Locksley, for he had been up and on his way before the break of dawn—and now he was nearing Tutbury town, where he would rest awhile at the old Dog and Partridge Inn for a bite and a sup with the host, one of his father's old retainers. Thus far he had not met a living soul. Following the river Dove, which joins the Trent below Tutbury, he would strike the Trent valley, due east for Nottingham town.

Presently he marched up High Street and stepped in through the little tap-room door of the white-and-black oak-timbered inn.

"Hulloa, whither goest thou, Master Robert, dressed all so gay and fine?" cried mine host of the Dog and Partridge.

"Knowest not, good Giles," quoth Robert, "of the shooting-match to be held on the morrow at Nottingham town? I go to shoot, with other stout yeomen, for the prize—a silver bugle."

"Saist thou so?" quoth Giles. "Marry, and it may be thou shalt win, for thou canst speed an arrow with the best; I know it well."

Then the worthy Giles called to his good dame for a hearty meal of the very best—nothing was too good for their master's gallant son. So they brought a leveret pasty, some fried trout, fresh from the river—a can of ale was too mean and coarse, it must be a flagon of wine, and that of the finest quality. So young Robert set to and made a hole in that pie that pleased the good dame mightily.

"Now, my brave young master," quoth Giles, "if thou thinkest to reach Nottingham town by nightfall thou must e'en away. The path is easy enow to Repton, but poor and boggy at Sawley; from thence, see to it thou leavest the Trent valley and dost

ROBIN HOOD

follow the upper woodlands. Then strike through the King's forest for the town."

So Robert parted from the worthy host and hostess of the Dog and Partridge with a full stomach and great store of good wishes. He marched down High Street of Tutbury town, looking neither to the right nor to the left while the townsfolk paused to stare at him and the maids glanced at him coyly, for they thought they never yet had seen a youth so fair. As for Robert, he recked nothing of their looks, for his mind was all set on the shooting-match at Nottingham. His head buzzed with pleasant thoughts of the morrow, and his blood coursed briskly through his veins. Soon he was swinging along the forest path at a five-mile gait. Yet as he jogged on he was alert, always prepared at a moment's notice to defend himself should harm threaten.

He knew full well his skill with the long-bow, for many a time in friendly trials he had beaten the King's foresters and the men of Locksley town. It was his fifteenth birthday on the morrow; he would surely win a prize, and after that—he pondered, and said to himself, "Mayhap I shall become one of the King's foresters, then an archer of the King's guard, and so off to the wars like my father before me."

Just at that moment he espied through the leafy glade a small herd of hinds and young fawns led by a broad-antlered hart passing slowly by beneath the branches of a wide-spreading oak. Instantly his bow was in place, with an arrow nocked to the string; but ere he loosed the shaft, he paused, bethinking himself of what might follow should he kill. He was sorely tempted, for he wished to make trial of his skill before to-morrow's test; yet in a moment he sighed, lowered his arm, and slacked his bow. He knew the penalty of killing the King's royal hart; not a soul that could bend a bow in all merry England but knew it well. Better by far to be shot and killed outright than to have both eyes torn from their sockets, and the forefinger and thumb cut from each hand, then to be led into the forest to bleed and die. And so, as he strode along, right glad was he that he had withheld his hand from slaying of the King's deer.

[9]

ROBIN HOOD

The sun was now at high noon. Since breakfast at the Dog and Partridge he had covered over twenty miles, and his stomach began to crave food. He made up his mind to rest awhile at the first spring or brook that lay in his path. At last he came to a little sparkling rivulet tumbling down a bank-side, where sat a swineherd.

"Ho, good fellow," cried Robert, "what news in these parts?"

"None that I wot of, my master, save that there be a shooting-match in the town on the morrow, and many, like thee, do wend their way to it. May our Good Lady grant thee a prize!"

"Grammercy, good man, so I trust she may."

Thereupon Robert sat down beside him, and taking from his pouch the brawn and bread, gave half to the swineherd, who swallowed it like a hungry dog, in big gulps, long before the youth had finished his share. Then, lying down at full length, Robert took deep draughts of the cold, clear water, and again started on his journey.

He had chosen to go afoot rather than on horseback because he could thus more easily make his way through the tangled mass of bracken and underbrush in the deep forest. This jaunt of over twoscore miles taxed his strength not at all, for he was both strong of limb and light of heart, and now, within half a dozen miles of Nottingham town, he was almost as fresh as when he had started. He had just heard the baying of a hound, when, as he came forth from a thick, tangled path to the open, a loud, angry voice shouted: "Hold! Who goes there that so boldly marches through the King's deer forest?"

The lad turned aside and saw a band of foresters seated and standing around the trunk of a giant oak. There were fifteen of them. All except the speaker were ranged round an immense dish of venison pie. Near by stood some barrels of ale. Leather wine-bottles and drinking-cups of horn lay scattered about on the mossy soft ground. All were dressed alike from top to toe in Lincoln green.

"My name is Robert Fitzooth," quoth Robert, boldly, "and

ROBIN HOOD

I go to the shooting-match at Nottingham town, where I hope to win a prize, and then, perchance, become a king's forester."

At this answer there arose a loud, boisterous laugh from every throat.

"What!" cried the chief, "thou a king's forester! Alack! thou couldst no more pull that man's bow hanging at thy back than could a blind kitten! Why, thou young whippet, our company needs men who can shoot a shaft from a goodly bow, not a babe just weaned."

"Do but look at him, comrades," said one, holding up a can of ale. "I trow a babe so young could never draw that string so much as the shake of a lamb's tail."

"I'll hold the best of you twenty marks," Robert made answer, turning red with anger and shame, "that I'll hit a mark at a hundred rods."

"Wilt thou so?" jeered the chief forester. "Lay down thy money."

"Alas! I have no money."

"O-ho! This young braggart hath no money, yet he layeth a wager! Come now, my fine bantam cock, what wilt thou wager?"

At this, young Robert went clean beside himself with rage.

"I lay my head against thy purse," he cried, in a choking voice, "whatsoe'er it contain, much or little, for there down the glade, fivescore rods away, I see a herd of deer, and by the leave of our Lady I will cause a hart to die."

"Done with you, and there is my purse," roared the angry forester; and he threw his purse on the ground among a pile of bows and quivers.

Now were the herd of deer in full view to all, led by a lordly hart which, turning, seemed to sniff some danger in the air. Then Robert took up his great bow, deftly tightened the string, nocked his shaft, and drew it to his ear.

"Remember, thou boaster, 'tis thy head is wagered," cried one; but Robert's hand trembled not, nor did his eye waver.

Twang! and the broad goose-feathered arrow flew through the air like a skimming swallow. All the foresters bent forward

ROBIN HOOD

eagerly, for they saw at once that the lad was no boaster, but as good an archer as themselves. The entire band were struck dumb when they beheld the great stag leap in the air, drop to its knees, and roll over with the arrow clean through its heart.

"The wager is mine," cried Robert, "were it a thousand pounds." Then he stepped forward to reach the purse.

"Hold!" thundered he who had lost the wager, amid the angry shouts of the foresters. "The wager thou hast won is the loss of thy two eyes. Thou art an outlaw, for thy arrow smote the King's hart royal, and all who do so must die." Thereupon they moved forward to encircle the lad, who stood ready with another shaft nocked to his bow-string.

"Beware!" said he. "He that draws one step nigher shall die like the hart."

Thereupon, one of the foresters, who had stealthily crept behind him, leaped upon his back and bore him to the ground with an arm about his neck.

"Now, by Saint Dunstan!" quoth the chief, "this naughty fellow hath come in happy time. Our good Sheriff of Nottingham hath taken it much amiss that we have brought no deer-stealers to court, though many have been killed from the coverts. He hath twice hinted that our time is spent in revels and feastings beneath the greenwood-trees. This likely tale, forsooth, will now be mended."

At this all laughed, and Robert's heart sank, but he lay still, biding his time. One lazy fellow, whose head was humming with ale, spake, and said:

"Marry, let us hang him on yon tall tree, and so an end."

"Nay, by 'r Lady, we owe the Sheriff a prize," quoth the chief.

"Ay, truly," said another. "We have need of the Sheriff's good-will. If ye will do as I rede you, let us bind him up in the skin of the royal hart he hath slain and sling him from our shoulders on a stout oak limb."

"Well said! That we will," cried they all.

So Robert was tied fast, hand and foot, with bow-strings, and carried to where the dead hart lay. When they had stripped

"REMEMBER, THOU BOASTER, 'TIS THY HEAD IS WAGERED"

ROBIN HOOD

away the hot skin with their keen hunting-knives and laid it flat on the greensward, they rudely threw him upon it and bound it with thongs over his body, leaving naught uncovered but his head. Robert's blood boiled, and he struggled with might and main to loosen the bonds which cut and pained him ever the more as he tried to free himself. Anon two strong fellows came, bearing a stout oak limb on their shoulders, to which the shapeless bundle was tied with rawhide thongs. Then they set off through the woodland, pushing their way amid thickets of young trees and stumbling over rough ground.

Robert was no great burden. Indeed, his body was but a plaything; yet the chief bade his men carry in turns, so that every one might have a chance to swing the living bundle from side to side against the trees as they passed. Always, in changing, the burden-bearers dropped their charge with a heavy thud to the ground, thinking to make him curse or groan. Much they marveled that he made no outcry, and some among the band whose hearts were softer than the rest felt pity that a brave lad should be so abused. As for Robert, he set his teeth and prayed inwardly. How different, thought he, was his present state from what it had been on that smiling May morn! He, who had thought to be an archer of the royal guard and to die at need for country and King, was to be killed without mercy as a felon. If the King could only know how his dastard foresters had lured a faithful subject with their taunts to a shameful death, it would fare ill with these same cruel knaves. He bethought him again and again of the tottering, sightless old man of his beloved Locksley town, whose tale of woe he had heard full oft. At last, what with the cramped and painful position in which he was tied and the heat of his body sweltering in the hide, his wits began to reel. His head dropped limp to one side and he knew no more.

"Hulloa!" cried a forester, "we've rocked our baby to sleep. Come, wake up, my young hedgehog." Then with rude thumps they sought to rouse him, but he awoke not.

The band had now left the forest and were treading the soft green turf of a meadow through which meandered a slow-running

ROBIN HOOD

stream. Just beyond the distant trees rose a church spire of a village where the foresters would doubtless rest and refresh themselves at the White Hart Inn. Drawing nigh the banks of the stream, the foremost of the two who bore the captive cried, "By my faith, this is a jolly place for a bath to revive our sleepy young blade."

"Thou saist truly," quoth the other; and with the words they dipped their burden into the stream. The cool water flowed over Robert's face and eyes, and he struggled, gasping, with dire fear in his heart; for he thought that now they would drown him, helpless, bound hand and foot, like a cat in a bag. But anon they lifted him out, and as he lay prone on the bank, scarce knowing whether he were alive or dead, he heard the low voice of one who had before shown some pity both by look and word.

"Nay, man," said the voice, "there is no need for that. To wet the burden will but make it the heavier. Let Steve and me take a turn."

"Ay, truly, Phil, our shoulders need a rest, and thou art young and lusty."

So Phil called a companion, who stepped forward from the band; and Robert's spirits rose to find some semblance of gentleness among these men, though truly he feared that this might be but a trick, to torment him further. But his doubts soon fled. As they moved along toward the village his sharp ear caught whispered words between his carriers.

"I' faith," said one, "I am aweary of this life—hard words and little pay!"

"What canst thou do, Phil?" the other made answer.

"With thy good help, Steve, we can save and avenge this brave young lad."

"Ay, so we might, but to what end?"

"Marry, to be free, to be our own masters and live a merry life under the greenwood-trees—above all, to save the life of one who may prove to be the best archer that ever bent bow."

These low-spoken words were sweetest music to Robert, who kept silent and waited till the time for action came. They had

ROBIN HOOD

now reached the village, and were within sight of the White Hart Inn. The men were weary and athirst, and the chief forester, nothing loath, gave them leave to rest, as they were still some distance from Nottingham town. In those days the inns and taverns were built with stables and outbuildings close to and facing the front entrance, the whole being entirely surrounded by a high stone wall, except the big oaken gates which led into the small courtyard. Into this yard the troop of foresters filed, with the prisoner carried by Phil and Steve in the rear.

"Shall we unbind the lad to stretch his limbs?" asked Steve.

"No, thou scurvy villain," roared the chief. "None but the Sheriff shall do the stretching. Lay him in the stable and guard him well. But hark'ee! We want no dead prisoner for our noble Sheriff, therefore put in his craw some oaten cake and a swill of water the while we quench our thirst with wine. Catching deer-stealers is dry work."

With that he strode through the little front door along a short passage into the big public chamber, and the rest followed him. In this room sat two sturdy fellows drinking ale. Both were armed, but their clothes showed them to be of the meaner sort of folk, though one was much the better clad. After giving orders for the best wine and food the chief turned to them, saying:

"What news, good fellows?"

"We know of none, your honor, save the shooting-match at Nottingham town on the morrow. Belike thou, too, goest thither."

"Oh, we have a saucy young rogue of a deer-stealer to be hung by our pious Sheriff—ay, and the best hand to shoot a shaft we've seen full many a day."

Then the foresters sat down to feast and sing a jolly lay, but the two others left the room. As they crossed the yard Phil accosted them, crying, "Good friend, wilt thou go within and beg the chief forester for a flagon of wine for the men on guard?"

"Marry, that will I," one of the strangers made answer, and straightway hastened to do as he was bid.

"Who is thy charge?" asked the other. Then, looking round,

he beheld in a corner the young lad trussed up in the skin. At that moment his companion returned with the wine, whereat Robert, catching sight of them, cried out of a sudden, "It is Giles and the swineherd!"

"Alack!" cried Giles. "Tell me what thou hast done, beloved son of my master, that was so happy and free this morn!"

Then Phil and Steve saw their chance and had hope of rescue. In hurried whispers the four debated.

"Let us haste, good comrades," said Giles, cutting the bonds with his sharp dagger. Then Robert got up from the ground with limbs stiff and sore, yet ready to do and dare any deed for his freedom. A plan was soon made. Phil and Steve with young Robert were to run outside the wall and through a little thatched cottage into a back garden, at the end of which flowed the stream. This stream, being too deep to ford, they must swim, pitching across their bows and quivers to keep them dry. In the forest, but a hundred rods away, they could make a stand behind the broad trunks of the friendly trees, to cover the escape of Giles and the swineherd should they be pursued. Meanwhile, Giles would quietly fasten the inn front door while his companion locked the big oak gates of the yard. Then, taking a light ladder used to climb the stable loft and placing it against the wall, Giles would get over and take the ladder with him.

Robert took up his bow and quiver, which the chief had meant to put in as evidence, along with the hide, before the Sheriff, and crept softly along the wall, Phil and Steve close behind him. He had stoutly refused at first to lead the way because of the extra risk to his friends. With his long-bow they knew he was no mean foe, but all were in the same plight, and he bent to their desire. All three were now safely outside the yard gate. The swineherd softly closed it, turned the big key round in the lock, and, taking it along, nimbly climbed the ladder. He dropped down lightly upon the other side and ran to follow the leaders.

In the mean time Giles was in great peril of his life, for he knew that as soon as he closed the front door the men inside would stop drinking and carousing. In his hand he held some of the

ROBIN HOOD

rawhide thongs that had bound Robert, with which he meant to tie fast the round iron handle to the latch. This, he hoped, would give him time to scale the wall. He now pulled the door —slowly at first, that the men within might not perceive the fading light in the passage. It was now half-way; every moment gave him comfort, for his companions were getting farther and farther away. He thought of his dead master, whose orphan son he wished to save, and said to himself:

"I never yet did repent of doing good, nor shall not now."

Silently and suddenly he closed the door and tied it fast. Straightway there arose a terrible uproar inside. The door was tried, kicked, and banged amid cries and oaths. But the stout rawhide thongs held, and Giles's foot was on the first rung of the ladder. He heard the angry chief shout, above the din, "To the windows, my lads! Shoot the traitors dead!"

Two foresters now crashed through the windows into the court-yard, and nocked their shafts. The bow-strings twanged, the arrows flew; but Giles was safe. He saw the top of the ladder pierced with arrows as it lay outside the high wall, and as he ran like the wind down the garden path he heard them thundering at the gate, shut in for the nonce, like rats in a trap. He knew that danger threatened him still as he plunged into the stream, swam across, and began to run along the meadows toward the forest. He heard a shout, and, turning, saw the swineherd, who could not swim, vainly searching a fording-place. Whate'er the danger, Giles was not the man to leave a comrade in distress. He went back again, crossed the stream, and then started afresh, swimming with the swineherd on his back. Just as he stretched forth his hand to the bank he heard the whizz of an arrow close by his ear; another, shot by the foremost forester, struck with deadly aim right at the back of the swineherd's neck, going through at the throat with such force as to pierce Giles's shoulder. With a scream the man tore the arrow from him, and Giles fell forward, with his companion lying beside him writhing in his last agony.

Recking naught of the danger, Robert sprang forth from the sheltering trees, and with set teeth, his eyes fixed on the deadly

ROBIN HOOD

marksman, chose a shaft and nocked it to the string. A dozen arrows came sailing over the meadows toward him, but they fell short by full twenty rods. He hesitated, standing there alone, with the bow half raised. He doubted not the trueness of his aim nor the strength of his bow, though the distance was great. Never before in all his happy boyhood had he wished for any man's death; yet the cruel treatment he had lately undergone from the very man who was now his target, hardened, for the moment, a naturally tender heart and burned to tinder all vestiges of forgiveness. As he thought how shamefully they had dealt with him, and how this very man had slain one of his friends, his face flushed with anger. He lifted his bow, drawing the shaft to its head. For a bare instant he hung at full stretch. Then with a loud twang the arrow sped. The chief, raising both arms, howled like a wolf, leaped forward, and fell flat on his face to the earth, with the arrow right through his heart.

The whole band of foresters were thunderstruck. Helpless to do aught against the young archer who so easily overshot them, they turned and fled, leaving their chief in his dying struggles on the ground. Steve and Phil now came from the forest, where they had waited, well assured that the lad would outshoot his pursuers. All three ran to the river-bank to succor Giles and the swineherd. Giles, who had but a glancing flesh-wound on his shoulder, had climbed up the bank and lay quite still, deeming that the foresters would think him dead. Robert then turned to the swineherd, whose lifeless body lay rigid in a pool of blood that had run from his throat, his mild blue eyes wide open. The sun had gone down in a blaze of glorious gold. The sky began to redden and turned to a cold purple gray. The long evening twilight had fallen. The moon and stars would soon be their only lamps.

Robert was sad at heart, and repented him sore of what he had done. With all his shooting he had never bethought him that he might as easily kill a man as a stag. He knew that men slew and were slain in fair fight, but the thought that he had taken a life was very bitter to him. As he watched his companions

ROBIN HOOD

tenderly carry away the limp, lifeless form that but an hour before had been so strong and lusty he wept and repeated time and again, "I, too, have killed a man." What the cruel chief had done, the crafty wager, the taunts at his skill and his youth, the unfeeling wish to win the Sheriff's favor through his torture, finally, the slaying of one of his generous rescuers—all these seemed now but poor excuses for his deed. So, though he had killed in hot blood and in defence of his life, it seemed to him that he would never again be blithe and care-free.

Sadly and silently they laid the body of the swineherd in the crevice of a rock and covered it with branches of oak, intending to return later and bury it. Each one muttered a prayer and turned away. Then, taking a path that led right into the depths of the forest, they were soon lost to view in the gathering darkness of the night.

III

ROBIN THE OUTLAW

Come listen to me, you gallants so free,
  All you that love mirth for to hear;
And I will tell you of a bold outlaw
  Who lived in Nottinghamshire.

**F**IVE years flew by, and Robert dwelt as an outlaw in the forest; but he no longer called himself Robert Fitzooth. Men knew him as Robin Hood. He was now twenty years old, scarce taller than of yore, but, from a slight, thin sapling of a youth, he had developed into a man broad of shoulder and deep of chest, with arms and legs of solid brawn and sinew. His hands and face were now deeply bronzed, and he had a short curly beard and a mustache of auburn red. Truly, he was a young man goodly to look upon, clad from head to foot in Lincoln green.

We last saw him and his companions cover the dead swineherd with leaves, and march, sad-hearted, into the deep forest. They knew full well that they must put many a mile betwixt them and the foresters, for when the Sheriff learned of what had happened he would set men and dogs upon their tracks. Then rewards would be offered to any who should make them captive and bring

[22]

ROBIN HOOD

them, alive or dead, to the court of the King. So they hasted through the forest, going northward, guided by the stars now faintly gleaming. Anon darkness came upon them, but by good-fortune they espied before them a charcoal-burner's hut, where they lay down and rested for the night. Before sunset of the next day they had reached Barnesdale Forest in Yorkshire, and here they dwelt awhile in peace, far away from the Sheriff and his men.

At this time King Henry had marched to the north with a great array to quell the Scotch Rebellion, and all four men joined the ranks as archers. Then, quitting the army, they journeyed north again to Plompton Forest, in Cumberland, where they bided for a space. King Henry was greatly troubled by the disobedience of his sons, Earl Henry and Richard, and his mind was ill at ease after the murder of Becket. That he might in some sort atone for it he made a pilgrimage to Canterbury, and there allowed himself to be scourged with a knotted cord by the priests. He spent a night in a dark crypt, and the next day rode, fasting, to London, where he fell ill of a fever.

At length Robin and his band became aweary of the cold northern winters and longed for their old haunts and companions. So they agreed to go back to the warmer lowlands. They had many adventures and narrow escapes by the way, but, keeping together in fair weather and foul, they made their way into Nottinghamshire and halted on the borders of Sherwood Forest hard by Newstead Abbey. Choosing a trysting-place surrounded by boggy land, with one narrow safe path leading from a clump of hazel bushes, they sallied forth in search of food and drink and other things of which they had need.

The little band was moving slowly along down a hillside. Though it was early in the day, yet was it hot and sultry.

"We shall have a storm before sundown," said one.

"Ay," quoth Giles, "and a heavy one, too, methinks."

While they spoke thus Robin said of a sudden: "Listen, comrades, there are strangers near by. I hear a lusty voice."

Standing still, they waited, listening, for they could see naught

ROBIN HOOD

through the maze of leafy trees. Anon they heard a loud voice close at hand. Robin led the way toward the sound, carefully treading the soft sward and hiding behind the trees. Soon they espied a group of foresters seated, with their backs to them, beneath a chestnut-tree, to which were bound two captives. They had often wished to add some stout followers to their company, and here, it seemed, was a chance. But how were they to free the captives? They agreed to bide until the two men were cut loose; so, lying down flat on the ground, each kept his eye fixed upon the scene before them. At last they grew weary.

"Phil," quoth Robin, "do thou steal round to yon tall elm and climb among its thick-branching leaves, then cry out, 'Help! Murder!' Then moan softly, while I creep along the other way nigh unto the captives."

Anon the cry was heard loud and clear in the silent woodland, and the foresters all started to their feet and ran forward, sore astonished, not knowing whence the sound came. Robin saw his chance as they rushed forth. Nimbly he sped toward the captives' tree and cut the thongs with his sharp dagger, saying, "Come quickly to freedom."

Giles and Steve, making a wide turn, joined them, and together they were soon out of the foresters' sight and hearing, and back to their chosen meeting-place. All were agreed that Phil was safe up in his tree. Yet, as the day wore on, their hearts misgave them. Just as they were planning to return in search of their comrade the storm burst forth in torrents of rain, with thunder and lightning. When it had passed they saw Phil come trudging along the little path over the bogs.

"Marry! Here am I," quoth Phil.

"Right welcome thou art. Tell us, good comrade, what hath befallen thee."

So they sat down in merry humor to listen.

"Well," began Phil, "when I had hid me in the tree, I shouted. Up rose the band, taking up their quarter-staffs and nocking their shafts as they rushed down. I was well covered, and they saw me not, but when they had beaten the woods well, yet found

ESPIED A GROUP OF FORESTERS AND TWO CAPTIVES

ROBIN HOOD

no sign of a living soul, I heard one say, 'Tis the foul fiend, and some one of us must surely die.' 'Nay,' quoth another, 'it was the cry of a man in sore distress. Then a third cried out, 'The foul fiend is truly about us. See! our prisoners have dropped into the bowels of the earth.' Forthwith they scampered back to find the hole where the fiend had taken the captives, yet they saw naught but the broken thongs. Then it behooved me to cry again to draw them away from following in thy tracks. So back they came to the tree, more bewildered than ever. Oh! how sore I pined to send a shaft among their addled pates, but that would end me, quoth I. With that the storm broke, and off they trudged through the rain to Nottingham town in sorry plight. But I lay still, snug and dry, till the rain stopped. Then down I came right gladly from my bower, and straightway came hither. An my eyes be not crooked and a-squint, ye have stout Tom Lee and Dick the Draper among you."

"Ay, here we are safe and sound, thanks to thee and thy friends. Right glad are we to meet so stout a band," quoth Dick.

Then said Robin, "It were well that these two lusty fellows, an it please them, should join with us."

Thereupon Tom Lee and Dick the Draper looked at each other and smiled.

"Nay, rather," quoth Dick, "come ye with me, for to say sooth we belong to a band of merry outlaws, as stout as ever drew bow, who dwell under the greenwood-trees in Sherwood Forest."

"No better life do I crave," quoth Robin, "than to be an outlaw in the green forest with brave and true men for comrades."

So they all followed Dick, who guided them through the pathless forest half a score of miles. Robin thought, as he strode along, that an outlaw's life had not been his choice, but it had been forced upon him, willy-nilly. A price was on his head, and he must either lose it or follow the life his comrades offered. Such a life need not be one of rapine and murder. He thereupon made a vow to do good deeds, so far as lay in his power. And that vow he kept through many a long year of forest life.

Dick led them deeper and deeper into the forest, and at

ROBIN HOOD

last they reached a small clearing of softest greensward, in the midst of which on a little hummock rose the trunk of a giant oak, hollowed out in the center, so that there was room within for a dozen stout yeomen to lie hid. In the hollow was a trap-door on the ground, which led by steps along a passage to the outlaws' treasure-store. At the back of the tree was a huge stone round tower with walls six feet thick—the remains of a Roman temple. It lacked both doors and windows, so that none might enter save by the trap. Another passage led from the treasure-store back to an outlet, in the forest, covered over by thick bushes.

A group of outlaws sitting and lying in the shade raised a shout of welcome to see their companions return safely with new friends. Then Dick and Tom told how they had been rescued from the foresters and who had done it. Robin Hood's skill as an archer was well known to them, and there was none in that country who thought not the better of him because he had put an end to the chief forester's brutal deeds. Dick wound his horn to draw the whole band together under the tree, and thus addressed them:

"Brother outlaws, so far we have done well and worked together without fear or favor in this our happy life. But I say we need and must have a captain and leader—one that is bold and the best archer in merry England. Therefore let us straightway set up a target, and he that shall prove the best marksman with gray-goose shaft, let him be our chief."

"Well said!" cried they all; and straightway they set up a target against a tree a hundred rods away.

"Nay," quoth Robin Hood, "that target is no test of an archer's skill. Let me place a target that is worthy of a stout bowman."

"That is but fair," cried the yeomen.

So Robin cut a six-foot hazel wand, set it upon the soft earth, and hung from it a garland of wild roses.

"The archer," cried Robin, "who sends his cloth-yard shaft through yon fair garland and touches not flower nor leaf at two

ROBIN HOOD

ROBIN HOOD

hundred rods away I call him worthy to be captain of this merry band." At that there fell a silence, and none stepped forward to make the test.

"If none other will shoot at this mark," quoth Dick the Draper, "do thou, good Robin, show our comrades what thou canst do."

Then Robin stepped forth with his great long-bow, nocked a shaft, and shot it clear through the garland so that neither leaf nor flower quivered so much as a hair's breadth.

"Do it again," cried Dick, "that it may seem to all no false shot."

"Ay!" quoth Robin, "and thrice again shall my arrow speed."

And thus it was that Robin Hood, amid jocund shouts, became the captain of the merry band of outlaws in Sherwood Forest. The fivescore outlaws seated themselves beneath the branches of the great oak, and Robin spake unto them.

"My merry men, all," quoth he, "as your captain and sworn leader I pray you to join me in a vow to spoil only our oppressors—sheriff or Norman baron, prior or abbot, knight or squire, any and all who grind and rob the poor. From such only will we take to help those who are needy, but to helpless women or children we will do no scathe."

Up rose the band with one accord and swore to obey and keep the vow. Then they fell to work to make ready a great feast, and the next fourteen days were set apart for feasting and merry sports. With wrestling-matches, bouts at quarter-staff, archery contests, bowling on the green turf, high jumping, and pole-leaping, the time passed blithely.

IV

ROBIN HOOD FIGHTS LITTLE JOHN

When Robin Hood was about twenty years old,
   With a hey down, down, and a down;
He happened to meet Little John,
A jolly brisk blade, right fit for the trade;
   For he was a lusty young man.

T last the great feast and merry sports were done. Then Robin said to his jolly bowmen: "This day I mean to fare forth to seek adventures. Mayhap I shall find some tall knight or fat abbot with an overfull purse." Picking out a few followers, he said to the rest: "Pray tarry, my merry men, in this our grove, and see that ye heed well my call, for should I be hard bestead I will sound three blasts on my horn, and then ye shall know that I am in dire need. So come to help me with all speed."

So saying, he wended his way with those he had chosen, to the outskirts of Sherwood Forest. At last they came to a meadow hard by a village, through which flowed a stream, little but deep.

"Bide here, my lads," quoth Robin, "behind these trees, while

"PRITHEE, GOOD FELLOW, WHERE ART THOU NOW?"

ROBIN HOOD

I go forth to meet yon tall fellow whom I see stalking forth this way."

So Robin started toward a long, narrow bridge made of a huge, flattened tree-trunk that spanned the brook. Now it chanced that both he and the stranger set foot upon the bridge at the same instant. They eyed each other up and down, and Robin said to himself, "This tall, lusty blade would be a proper man for our band, for he stands nigh seven foot high, and hath a mighty frame." Then, to test if the fellow's valor were equal to his height, bold Robin sturdily stood and said: "Get off the bridge and give way. Dost thou not see there's no room for both to cross?"

"Get off thyself, thou saucy knave, or I'll baste thy hide with my staff," the stranger replied.

Then Robin drew from his quiver a long, straight shaft and fitted it to his bow-string.

"Thou pratest like an ass," quoth he. "Ere thou couldst strike me one blow I could send this goose-winged shaft through thy heart."

"None but a base coward would shoot at my breast while I have naught but a staff in my hand to reach thee."

At this Robin lowered his bow and thrust the shaft back into the quiver. "I scorn thee," he said, "as I do the name of a coward, and to prove that I fear thee not let me lay by my long-bow and choose a tough staff of ground-oak from yonder thicket. Then here upon this narrow bridge we will fight, and whosoever shall be doused in the brook shall own himself beaten."

The tall stranger replied, "That suits me full well to a dot, and here will I abide till thou comest."

Then bold Robin strode off to the thicket, where he cut and trimmed a trusty, knotted six-foot staff. Sooth to say, the more he looked upon the stranger the less he relished coming to blows with him, for he thought he had never seen a sturdier knave. None the less he stepped upon the bridge and began to flourish his staff above his head right bravely. With watchful eyes and careful tread both stepped forward till they met in the middle.

[35]

ROBIN HOOD

In a trice Robin gave the stranger a crack on his broad neck that made his bones ring like stones in a tin can; but he was as tough as he was big, and he said naught but, "One good turn deserves another." With that he whirled his great staff faster and faster, bringing it down on Robin's guard with such a rain of blows that one would think twenty men were at it. Both played so rapidly and the blows were so deftly struck that neither one after half an hour's battle seemed to gain a whit. Robin tried all his skill in parrying and feinting, but he could do no more than give the stranger a whack on his ribs and shoulder which only made him grunt. As he began to grow weary the other laid on the faster, so that Robin's jacket smoked with many a thwack and he felt as if he were on fire.

At last he got a crack on the crown that caused the blood to flow down his cheek, but he only fought the more fiercely and pressed on so hard that the stranger slipped and nigh fell over. But he regained his footing, and with a furious onslaught he brought his staff down with such tremendous force that he smashed Robin's staff into smithers and toppled him with a great splash full on his back into the brook.

"Prithee, good fellow, where art thou now?" quoth the stranger.

"Good faith, in the flood," quoth Robin, "and floating along with the tide."

Thereupon he waded the stream and pulled himself up on the bank by an overhanging branch. He sat him down, wet to the skin, and laughingly cried, "My brave soul, thou hast won the bout, and I'll no longer fight with thee." So saying, he set his horn to his lips and blew a loud blast, whereat the stout yeomen came running forth from behind the trees.

"Oh, what is the matter, good master?" they cried. "Thou art as wet as a drown'd rat."

"Matter or no matter," quoth Robin, "yon tall fellow hath in fighting tumbled me into the brook."

"Seize him, comrades, for in the brook he shall likewise go to cool his hot spirit," said one.

"Nay, nay, forbear," cried Robin, "he is a stout fellow. They

[36]

ROBIN HOOD

shall do thee no harm, my tall friend. These bowmen are my followers, with three score and nine others, and if thou wilt, my jolly blade, thou shalt join us and be my good right-hand man. Three good suits of Lincoln green shalt thou have each year and a full share in all we take. We'll teach thee to shoot the fat fallow deer, and thou shalt eat sweet venison steak whene'er thou wilt, washed down with foaming ale. What saist thou, sweet chuck?"

The stranger replied, "Here is my hand on't, and with my whole heart will I serve so bold a leader, for no man living doubteth that I, John Little, can play my part with the best. But on one condition will I join your band."

"And what may that be?" quoth Robin.

"It is that ye show me an archer who can mend a shot I shall shoot with stout long-bow and arrow."

"Well, thou shalt shoot," quoth Robin, "and we will mend thy shot if we may." So saying, he went and cut a willow wand about the thickness of a man's thumb and, peeling off the skin, set it up before a tree fivescore paces away. "Now," quoth he, "do thou choose a bow to thy liking from among all my men, and let us see thy skill."

"That will I, blithely," quoth John. Choosing the stoutest bow and straightest arrow he could find among a group lying on the sward, he took most careful aim, pulling the arching bow to its utmost stretch. The arrow flew, and lodged with its point right through the wand. "A brave shot!" cried the archers all.

"Canst thou mend that, bold outlaw?" asked John.

"I cannot mend the shot, but I'll notch thy shaft in twain." So saying, Robin took his bow, put on a new string, and chose a perfect, straight arrow with gray goose feathers truly tied. Then, bending the great bow, he let fly the shaft. For a moment the archers watched, breathless; then, with shouts of glee, they saw the stranger's arrow split fairly in twain.

"Enough," quoth John. "Never before have I seen so true an eye guide a shaft. Now I know an archer fit to serve."

All cried out that he had said well, and then in right merry mood they started back to their forest home, there to feast and christen their new comrade. The rest of the outlaw band gave them a joyful welcome, and soon brought in a brace of fat does roasted to a nut-brown color, with casks of humming strong ale. When all were seated 'neath the friendly shade of the great oak, Robin placed John beside him, and they all feasted to their hearts' content, with song and merry jest, and oft Robin told the tale of the great fight on the bridge.

"And now, my jolly companions, let us have the christening," quoth he, at last.

So they made big John sit down, and seven archers formed in a circle round him. Then a bald-headed yeoman offered to act the part of priest. He came forth holding up a tankard of ale, and asked:

"What name shall we call this pretty sweet babe?"

As no one spake, he answered himself.

"This infant," quoth he, "was called John Little, but that name we shall change anon. Henceforth, wherever he goes, not John Little, but Little John shall he be called."

The liquor was then poured over John's head, trickling down his face; and so they baptized him. With shouts of laughter that made the forest ring, in which Little John merrily joined, the christening came to an end with sweet song and jocund jest.

Then Robin took Little John to the treasure chamber and gave him a suit of Lincoln green and a great bow of yew.

V

WILL GAMWELL BECOMES WILL SCARLET

RIGHT glad was Robin Hood that he had gotten so bold and trusty a blade for his comrade. He wanted no braver friend to stand beside him in fight, nor merrier heart to play and feast withal. As for the rest of the merry men, they loved Little John well, and all stood in awe of his great strength. For in the whole band was none that might withstand him in a bout with the quarter-staff, nor, saving only Robin, was there such another archer in all the land. So Little John became Robin's right-hand man, and they loved each other like brothers. Such a pair of bold spirits were equal to a troop, and in sooth the King's men, knowing full well the outlaws' strength and the deadly aim of their shafts, wisely kept many miles away from their trysting-place.

Of hiding-places Robin had full many, scattered far and wide, which his men found as they went back and forth through the forest. Whenever they chanced upon a fit place, were it cave or bower, Robin called the band together, and all fell to work with a will, clearing and building, to make a forest home good for winter or summer. None molested them, for their name and fame were

ROBIN HOOD

known throughout the land, and most people thought it best to keep to the great highway or little lanes between the towns and villages rather than to journey through the forest with a chance of being robbed for their pains. Moreover, the country-folk held Robin in high esteem, for they knew him to be the friend of the poor.

It happened one day at noontide that Robin called to Little John and said: "Our larder is low. We will together seek to replenish it. To Ermine Street we will go, for, peradventure, we may meet with some fat abbot or mayhap a stout foe. Do thou get thy trusty staff, and I will don my sword and buckler in case of need." So with their good long-bows hanging at their sides they started off through the forest. Anon they came to a path which led to a lane that went curving up to a hill, at the top of which stood the castle walls of a neighboring knight.

Quoth Little John, "Look who cometh down the lane."

"Marry," quoth Robin, "a gay spark, indeed! Truly his raiment is of so hot a color, methinks there is danger he may set the woods afire."

The stranger wore a doublet of silk, and hose of bright scarlet; he carried a long-bow, with a sword and buckler at his side. Glancing from side to side as he came, he perceived down a narrow woodland path a herd of deer leisurely pass by. Robin and Little John watched him as he quickly bent his long-bow and slew the best of all the herd at forty rods away.

"He shooteth fair enough," quoth Robin. "Yet by 'r Lady, I like not these gaudy popinjays. Do thou, good comrade, hide behind yon thicket while I step forth and speak him fair."

With that Little John strode away to hide; and Robin marched up to the stranger, who now stood bending over the great hart lying dead at his feet.

"Marry," quoth Robin, "who gave thee leave to kill the deer in this forest?"

The scarlet stranger turned not aside and answered never a word. Again Robin spake.

"How now, gay spark, art thou dumb?"

ROBIN HOOD

"And what is that to thee, good fellow? Pass on. I have no need of thee, and I like not thy clattering tongue. Go thy ways whence thou camest."

This answer nettled Robin and stirred his blood, for the fellow spoke insolently as to one beneath him. "Marry, come up," quoth Robin. "It is my wont to take toll of all who come this way. Therefore thou shalt either give me thy purse or else thou shalt not pass."

"And who art thou that dost threat me so boldly?" sneeringly asked the stranger.

"I am the King of Sherwood Forest, and all in these parts do obey me."

"Nay, good friend, king or no king, I care not for thee or for aught that thou canst do. Therefore, pass on, unless perchance thou cravest a buffet of my fists."

At these words Robin cried, "Were I to blow my horn I have those who would help me to make thee do whatever I wish."

"Ah! then," replied the stranger, "with my good broadsword would I put to flight a-many such as thee." With that the gaily dressed fellow disdainfully turned his back and bent down, feeling the antler's prongs. He seemed to think that Robin had gone.

Then, to make a test of this outwardly brave show, Robin drew his bow, pointing the shaft straight on the stranger's heart.

"How now, thou villain," cried the other, "what woulds't thou?"

"By Saint Dunstan," quoth Robin, angrily, "I would take thy purse, and make thee pay toll for that saucy tongue of thine."

"Ah, well, as to that, take it and welcome." Then, making believe to unlace his pouch, he quickly got his long-bow before him and stood boldly facing Robin with his shaft pointed to kill.

"Hold! Hold thy hand!" exclaimed Robin. "It were vain for both to shoot and each to slay the other. I have a mind that one should be the victor. Let us take our broadsword and bucklers and under yon tree try which of us be the better man."

"As I hope to be saved." quoth the stranger, "I will not flee one foot."

[43]

ROBIN HOOD

No sooner were the words spoken than they strode off to a level sward under the branches of a beech-tree. Both calmly made ready for battle, each fastening his buckler upon his left arm. Soon they were wielding their broad blades with a right good will, and the woods rang with the sound as sword clashed on shield. As the fight grew hot each perceived in the other a tough and skilful foe. With a keen eye Robin watched the stranger, who guarded himself well, warding off many a stout blow that otherwise would have drawn blood, making his skin the color of his scarlet doublet. At last Robin gave him a clout which glanced from his buckler, just missing his ear, and nipping off a long red plume from his cap. The scarlet stranger grew more wary. He waited, parried and feinted, then drew back, and of a sudden leaped forward again. As he leaped he struck, beating down the buckler, which but partly turned the blow. The sword cut a long gash across Robin's skull, making the blood trickle down from every hair of his head and blinding his eyes so that he could no longer see to fight.

"God-a-mercy, good fellow," quoth Robin, "tell me truly who and what thou art. Fain would I know thy name."

"My name is Will Gamwell," answered the stranger, "and I was born and bred in Maxwell town. I seek mine uncle, who dwelleth in these parts. Some do call him Robin Hood."

At this, bold Robin jumped from the ground on which he lay, and cried, "Art thou, indeed, young Will Gamwell, mine own dear cousin,* with whom I played as a boy?"

"What, art thou Robin Hood? Then I am indeed thine own sister's son, and sore I do repent me of the wound I gave thee, for I knew thee not. But now right glad am I that I have found thee. And art thou in good sooth the famous Robin Hood? Good faith, little did I think to hold mine own against so stout a man. Truly had not fortune favored me, I know right well I should now be lying stretched upon earth, and not thou."

"Nay," quoth Robin, "the blow was fairly struck, and thou art the stoutest fellow of thy hands that ere I coped withal. As for the wound, it is but a scratch."

[44]

*Here the words cousin and coz denote kinship, rather than meaning the child of an aunt or uncle.

"GOD-A-MERCY, GOOD FELLOW," QUOTH ROBIN, "FAIN
WOULD I KNOW THY NAME"

ROBIN HOOD

Thereupon they embraced and kissed each other on both cheeks.

Meanwhile Little John had seen his master fall and the stranger bend over him, but had never dreamed that he was wounded until he failed to rise. Then, dashing forward, he shouted, "Give me thy sword, my master. We will see if he can beat me."

"Nay, nay," cried Robin, "hold thy hand, Little John, for this same tall youth is none other than my sister's son, Will Gamwell, and he shall be one of our merry band."

Little John thereupon changed his tone, and turned to greet the new-found cousin with a hearty handshake and a right good hug of welcome to his broad chest. For Little John's heart, like his body, was big, and the three were soon on the best of terms. Then and there a love grew up between them which lasted many a long year. Arm in arm, with the mighty Little John in the middle, they started off to find a cool spring or rivulet to bathe Robin's still bleeding wound. This done and Robin's pate bound up with a piece of linen, they strode along a fern-lined path, with the great dead hart slung from the brawny back of Little John.

"Come now," quoth jolly Robin, "tell me, good nephew, how it befell that thou didst leave thy home and come to seek me, an outlawed man, in the forest; for methought thou hadst house and lands enough."

"That will I, blithely," quoth young Gamwell. Then he told how, when his father died and he fell heir to the estate, a dastard Norman baron whose lands lay anigh his had plotted with his father's old steward to slay him that the lands might be his. So the steward, being bribed with a great sum, gave his word. On a day young Will was hunting in the forest when he spied the old rascal with bow bent and shaft pointed at his breast.

"And so without more ado," quoth Will, "I got me behind a tree and shot him where he stood. Then was I made an outlaw for killing a man, and straightway betook myself to the forest to seek out my good uncle. For, in faith, they are fain to walk

ROBIN HOOD

in wood who may not walk in town. And now thou knowest all."

Then said Robin: "In happy time thou comest, fair coz, and I thank the saints that this day I have escaped with my life from the stoutest swordsman in England, found a dear nephew, and gained a brave comrade for my merry men."

Soon they reached their trysting-place, and much the outlaws wondered to see bold Robin with a cloth about his head and a tall stranger in scarlet beside him. But when they knew who Will Gamwell was and how stoutly he had fought with Robin, they welcomed him gladly.

"Go now," said Robin to Will, "I long to see thee dressed as one of our band; so get thee a change of good Lincoln green in place of that most fiery raiment, which shall not be forgotten. Since the law is on thy head and name, that name shall hereafter be Will Scarlet. And next to Little John here, thou shalt be my right-hand man."

Anon Will Scarlet returned dressed all in Lincoln green. All were hungry, and straightway they spread a great feast on the soft greensward. Robin sat at the head, with Little John on his right and his nephew, now Will Scarlet, on his left. The great haunch of smoking-hot venison was always placed before Little John to do the carving. Other dishes there were—roast geese, ducks and swans, grouse, partridges, pastry pies of rabbits, hares, and squirrels. Then came salmon and trout from the rivers, and great pikes from the ponds and lakes—some boiled, others roasted and stuffed. In good sooth, the outlaws had no lack of meat and drink. The broad forest was their domain, and all its creatures were theirs for the taking. From time to time great tubs of wine and barrels of nut-brown ale were brought by pack-horses to a certain spot, to be carried thence by the outlaws to their trysting-place. All fared alike, and all were well fed, summer and winter.

As for Will Scarlet, he was at first amazed, then wondrous glad to have found a life so goodly and free from care. While the merry jests went round he, at Robin's request, told how his life

MASTER WILL SCARLET

ROBIN HOOD

had been spent and what troubles he had passed through since both were boys together. Robin's thoughts went back to his old home by Needwood Forest; but he had no real desire to leave the greenwood, and he knew full well that such a thing might not be. An outlaw he had been since his fifteenth year, and an outlaw he must remain till the breath left his body.

VI

ROBIN HOOD WINS THE GOLDEN ARROW

O**N a fine morning a sennight after the merry
feast in honor of Will Scarlet you might have
seen a tall fellow dressed in ragged clothes
striding through the forest toward the outlaws' bower. As he came nigh the great oak
he gave a call like the hoot of an owl. Some
of the band heard him, and hooted in turn.

"'Tis the call," quoth one, "of our worthy spy—the honest
servant of the Sheriff's house, that hath news to tell of what goes
on in Nottingham town."

Striding forth from the trees into the open glade came the
ragged spy.

"What news hast thou, Tom o' Clayton?" asked Robin.

"Brave news, good outlaw," quoth he, "for his worship the
Sheriff hath hied him to London town with a troop of his retainers all dressed in gay attire and made complaint to King
Henry and Queen Eleanor of the great scathe done his good name
and chattels by one Robin Hood and his outlaw band."

"And what said the King?" asked Robin.

"The King was sore wroth, as I have heard tell. 'Why,' quoth
he, 'what wouldst thou that I should do? Art thou not sheriff

ROBIN HOOD

for me? The law is in force, therefore do thou execute it as is thy bounden duty. Get thee gone and sweep the forest clear of all these thieving rogues, or, by my golden crown, thou art no sheriff for me.' Then was the Sheriff sorely troubled and crest-fallen, and he left the court with a fiery-red face amid the laughter of all the King's attendants. And now he hath proclaimed a great shooting-match to be held in fair Nottingham town three days hence, with a prize of a cunningly wrought arrow with a golden head and shaft of white silver."

With that stepped forth a brave yeoman, young David of Doncaster. "Master," he said, "be ruled by me, and let us not stir from the greenwood. This same match is but a wile of the Sheriff's to entrap thee. The shrewd old rogue thinks to get us all together in the town and so to take us unawares."

Quoth Robin: "Thy words do not please me, for they savor of cowardice. With bow and staff and good broadsword we may match the Sheriff and all his base churls. Natheless, good David, thou saist truly, 'tis a crafty plan—but we will meet guile with guile. Let us all disguise ourselves and be clad as common yeomen, tinkers and tanners, beggars and friars. If we scatter and mix in the crowd none shall know that outlaws be among them. But let each take care to have a stout coat of chain mail beneath his jerkin."

Then up spake brave Little John. "The plan I like full well. What say ye, my comrades?"

"With right good will," cried every one, right lustily.

"Then make ye ready, my merry men all," quoth Robin Hood. "I, with tattered scarlet coat and black patch over one eye, will shoot my best for this same golden arrow, and if I win we shall keep it in our bower as a trophy."

So on that bright sunshiny morning early, they made ready with shouts of laughter, for in such strange guise were they tricked out that scarce any man could name his neighbor. Some had dyed their beards, and all doffing their garb of Lincoln green had donned raiment that suited them full ill. Truly such a

[53]

ROBIN HOOD

gathering of tall, lusty beggars, tinkers, friars, and men of all trades was ne'er before seen in Sherwood Forest.

The little birds caroled; the titlark and goldfinch, the green linnet and spotted thrush, sang from every bush and tree as the merry company started forth from their leafy bower with hearts all firm and stout, each resolving that, should he fall foul of the Sheriff's men, he would clout their pates with right good will. Anon they left the forest in different places by threes and fours, that none might get an inkling of their purpose to be present at the butts. Every street and every little lane was dotted with a mixed crowd—mostly afoot, though here and there a knight rode by with his proud dame by his side or a haughty abbot astride his sleek cob, disdainful of the poorer folk that louted low as he passed. Many strangers could be seen with their bows slung at their sides, dust-covered and tired, who were on their way to this famed trial of skill. So Robin and his band mingled with the people that journeyed toward Nottingham.

The shooting range—or butts—lay outside the town on a level field of green turf, flanked on one side by sloping banks, where the poorer people sat on the grass. On the other side, shaded from the sun's rays, were benches and a gallery set apart for the Sheriff, his wife, and other officers of the town. Here, too, sat barons and knights with ladies fair, dressed in state and decked in colors gay. The stands were trimmed in bright draperies, buntings, ribbons, and flags, and were guarded by men-at-arms with hauberks and spears. Heralds with trumpets stood ready to announce the beginning of the sports.

The field was crowded early, long before the great folk arrived, for you must know it had been noised abroad that the Sheriff had gathered together a large troop of the King's foresters, besides his own men, that he might the better take Robin Hood and his fellow-outlaws. The beautiful and costly prize had brought many famous archers from neighboring counties. From Tutbury, Stoke, and Stafford came the well-known Ned o' Tinkersclough, Simon of Hartshill, and Roger o' Thistlebery—the latter a brawny blacksmith from Newcastle who had ne'er been

ROBIN HOOD

vanquished. From Derbyshire came two stout archers named Ralph of Rowsley and Hugh o' the Moors—both confident to bear away the prize. So everybody was on tiptoe awaiting what might betide. Some feared a battle, but many there were among the poor and lowly who hoped to see the Sheriff's men soundly drubbed.

All the outlaws save Robin Hood scattered through the crowd and none knew them. The Sheriff, when he had taken his seat, signaled the herald to sound three blasts as a warning to the archers to be prepared, and then the rules were proclaimed, that every one might understand them. All was now ready, the silver horn again sounded three blasts, and the archers began to shoot. The Sheriff looked anxiously round about, peering from side to side, first at the archers and then at the crowd.

"Ah," quoth he, scratching his head, "I see none in Lincoln green, such as the outlaws are wont to wear. I weened he would have come, for it is little like Robin Hood to bide at home when there is fair sport toward. Nay, rather would he risk his head. Yet perchance he feareth."

Calling a trumpeter to him, he said, "Dost thou see Robin Hood among these archers?"

"Nay, truly I see him not, your worship. Those that foot the line are all well known to me. Moreover, the bold outlaw's beard is golden as the setting sun, yet none here hath a beard save the ragged stranger in scarlet with but one eye—and his beard is dark brown."

"He durst not come, and is a cowardly knave," murmured the Sheriff.

Meanwhile, the ragged man in red stood up beside the crowd of archers without a fear and waited till most of the men had shot. The four targets surrounding the small one in the center were well covered and spotted with shafts, yet none had hit the inner circle. The great throng applauded, for such shooting was seldom seen. Already a goodly number had dropped out, leaving but five archers, Roger o' Thistlebery, Hugh o' the Moors, two strangers, and the ragged red one with the black eye. At the

[55]

ROBIN HOOD

third round Roger planted his shaft but the breadth of a groat from the center.

"That shot can ne'er be mended," roared the Sheriff, rising from his seat. "The man from Stafford wins the prize unless yon ragged robin redbreast shall outdo him, which is scarce likely sithen he hath but one eye."

He of the black eye and red coat never looked toward the Sheriff.

"A fair shot, Roger," quoth he. "Hadst thou but allowed for the slight breeze thy shaft would have pinked the clout."

Hugh o' the Moors came next, and he saw the wisdom of what the stranger had said. So, taking good heed of the wind, he let go the string with a twang, and his arrow pierced the very center. Thereat the people shouted and then fell silent of a sudden as the one-eyed archer took up his great bow and with seeming carelessness let fly his shaft. Then, gaping with open mouths and eyes, they saw Hugh's arrow fall to the ground split to pieces, and the stranger's shaft lodged right in its place.

"Red-coat wins; Red-coat hath the prize," they cried. Then, surging forward, they half dragged, half carried the winner in front of the Sheriff's stand, where the fair ladies cheered and waved their ribbons.

"And now, brave archer," quoth the Sheriff, "here is the prize thou hast fairly won. Thine eye is true, and bearing bold. Where dost thou hail from, and what name dost thou go by?"

"From Locksley town I come, and Nat the Blinker am I called."

"Well, Nat, though thou canst only blink with one eye, thou art the best archer my two eyes have ever seen. Surely thou needest a better coat. If thou wilt serve me and enter my company, I will make thee captain, with good pay, enough to eat and drink, and a chance to capture that knavish thief, Robin Hood, who loved his hide too well to venture here this day. Come now, by Saint Hubert, is it a bargain?"

"Nay," quoth the man in scarlet. "No master will I serve."

"Then out upon thee, thou saucy fellow! Get thee gone ere my men whip thee from out the town. Thou art a fool or else

AN ARROW CAME WHIZZING THROUGH THE OPEN
WINDOW

thou art a knave. I have a mind to put thee in a dungeon cell to cool thy hot blood, and so would I do but that thou hast pleased me with thy shooting."

So the tattered stranger turned away and, mingling with the crowd, was seen no more.

The sun was setting behind the great oak in the forest glen, and the balmy evening air was tinged with the savory smell of roast venison and great steaming game pies that lay on the ground amid barrels and tankards of foaming nut-brown ale. Surrounding this great feast sat the merry band of outlaws, ready to begin carving with their sharp daggers, when a tattered stranger in scarlet appeared, bearing in his hand an object that all might see. Then a mighty shout was heard that echoed through the forest:

"Welcome and long life to our dear captain, brave Robin Hood that won the prize."

So Robin Hood brought the arrow of silver and gold to Sherwood Forest.

The feast was a jolly one. All had merry jests to tell of what they had done in the strange garb they wore, for they knew many that knew them not, and in sooth their own fathers would have passed them by. So with songs and jollity the joyous feast went on till the stars began to peep; and the outlaws, like the birds, went to roost before night's mantle wrapped the leafy trees in darkness. But before they dispersed Robin said to Little John:

"I like not the Sheriff's words, and fain would I have him know that it was Robin Hood to whom he gave the prize."

"Ah!" quoth Little John, "that would be sour mash to his crop, but how to do it passeth my wits. Yet hold, I have it." And for a time he spake earnestly with Robin Hood, who laughed aloud and clapped him upon the back.

On the morrow, as the Sheriff sat at his meal at the head of a long table of guests, he spake loud in praise of the shooting. "But sore grieved am I," quoth he, "that Robin Hood was not—"

ROBIN HOOD

As that last word came from his lips an arrow came whizzing through the open window, landing right in the breast of a fat capon that lay on the table. The Sheriff and his guests started up in dismay at so strange a sight.

"What means this—a plot or treason?" roared the Sheriff.

Then in a calmer tone he bade an attendant get the shaft and bring it to him. As he took it up he saw a strip of bark wrapped around it, which he straightway tore off and unwound. Within was writing, and, with staring eyes, he read:

"It was Robin Hood that bore away the golden arrow."

Then the Sheriff dropped to his chair in a limp mass, crying:

"The crafty villain hath again covered me with shame and sorrow! What am I to do? What can I do? It was that black patch on his evil eye that deceived me. I felt in my bones none but that saucy knave would beard me so." Then, bringing down his fist with a bang upon the table and breaking the arrow to splinters, he cried, "By the bones of Saint Swithin, I will patch his other eye—yea, both eyes, that are much too keen for my peace. When I do catch him I will stretch his neck the length of a goose."

VII

HOW ROBIN HOOD MET FRIAR TUCK

FOR a time after the winning of the golden arrow the merry outlaws kept them close in Sherwood Forest. When the larder was well supplied with game the great oak glade was given up to sport. Some would play at bowls, or at dice; others would have wrestling-matches, bouts at quarter-staff, or mock duels with sword and buckler. But their favorite and never-ending delight was shooting with the long-bow—that trusty weapon which made them so justly famed and feared.

Will Scarlet, being the last to join the band, had many friendly challenges to stand up against. He knew his own skill, as likewise did Robin Hood and Little John, but many others wished to put him to the test. In all these contests Will acquitted himself honorably. One day Little John took a bow-string and hung up a dead squirrel from a bough at five hundred feet away, and after taking careful aim, because the wind swayed the mark, he sped his shaft clean through the squirrel's body amid resounding cheers.

"God's blessing on thy head," quoth Robin. "Gladly would I walk a hundred miles to see one that could match thee."

At that Will Scarlet laughed full heartily.

"That is no such hard matter," quoth he, "for at Fountains Abbey there dwells a curtal friar that can beat both him and thee."

ROBIN HOOD

Then Robin leaped up lightly from the greensward, where he had been lying stretched at length.

"Now, by 'r Lady," quoth he, "neither food nor drink will I touch until I have seen this friar of thine, were he in very truth a hundred miles away. Therefore make ready to lead us, while I don my cap of steel, broadsword, and buckler, to meet this holy archer."

"It be no hundred miles, good uncle," quoth Will. "We shall gain Fountains Abbey ere noon."

So Little John, Will Scarlet, and Robin strode through the forest at a quick gait, mile after mile without a stop, till they came to Needwood Forest, hard by Tutbury, where Friar Tuck had in days past received Will Scarlet to his broad bosom, learned to love him, and taught him all his skill with sword and long-bow and quarter-staff. Fountains Abbey was so called from a sparkling silver rivulet that danced down the moss-grown, fern-lined rocks, at the side of which the Friar had built a hermitage of rocks and boulders carried from a brook close by. Here he dwelt alone—cool and sheltered in summer, warm and snug in winter. In such a place a man might fast and pray undisturbed, or perchance drink good wine and feast upon the dun deer, if he liked better; for there was none to say him nay. From time to time a wandering knight on his war-horse, or pious abbot on an ambling pad, caught a glimpse in passing of the little forest abode, and would there alight for a drink at the sparkling fountain and a blessing from the Friar. But Friar Tuck held aloof from all save the few he chose as friends, and among them was the young curly-headed lad Will Gamwell, whose estates ran hard by the forest.

When the three outlaws were still some way off they caught sight of Fountains Abbey, below them, through a slight opening of the trees.

"There," quoth Will Scarlet, "thou wilt find the holy man thou seekest."

"Well," said Robin, "do ye two remain here. I fain would parley with this man alone."

ROBIN HOOD

"Nay, that we will not," Little John replied. "Thou art always over-ready to put thy head in danger without a cause."

"Truly, as to danger from a holy man I have no fear," said Robin, "but I would have my way in this."

So saying, he strode forward alone, leaving Little John and Will behind, till a blast from his bugle should call them. He trudged along till he came to a brook, by the side of which, seated upon the ground among a bunch of tall ferns, he espied a man with a missal book on his lap and a leather bottle at his lips in the act of drinking. So long the bottle remained tilted in air that Robin stole anigh ere the other saw him. Robin stood still, and the bottle was slowly lowered, displaying a perfectly round, fat face as red as a cherry, with small, laughing blue eyes fringed with heavy black eyebrows. The friar's shaven crown shone like glass, and it too was fringed with a circlet of curly black hair. His broad, fat neck was quite bare, and back of it was a cowl of rough, brown cloth attached to a loose, flowing robe of the same stuff, covering a powerful and strong-limbed body. Round his middle was buckled a leathern belt that held some keys, a string of beads, and a dagger. Beside him on the ground lay a sword, a buckler, and a steel cap.

As he slowly took the bottle from his lips he beheld the stout yeoman standing there, and straightway such a look of amazement came over his funny red face that Robin burst forth into a loud, hearty laugh. "Holy man," quoth he, "methought that bottle was glued to thy face, so long and lovingly did it cling to thy cherry lips. If there be aught left within it, the draught must be right pleasant. I would fain drink thereof, to sweeten my dry throat withal."

"Ah! wouldst thou?" was the answer. "Then why not test yon cool, sparkling brook from whence the bottle was filled?"

"Nay, nay, good Friar, thou wouldst make no such pretty gurgling music with water as I heard from thee but now. What is more, gin thy rosy cheeks belie thee not, precious little water hath passed thy lips this many a day."

"Well," said the Friar, "a pious man ought not to deny a

[63]

ROBIN HOOD

stranger who asks a drop to quench his thirst." So saying, he passed the bottle to Robin.

Robin took a long pull and found the liquor so good that he tipped the bottle higher and higher, keeping it so long tilted upright that at last the Friar jumped to his feet with a roar like a bull, saying:

"Thou greedy guts, thou tap without end, by Saint Wilfrid I will part thy mouth and my bottle with a cuff over thy ribs that will land thee on the other side of the brook!"

"Ay," quoth jolly Robin, smacking his lips, "right good Rhenish water, I trow! Grammercy for the loan of thy bottle, which I will straight refill from the brook for thy future use."

"Nay, mock me not," cried the Friar, peering anxiously down the neck of the bottle, "but go thy ways while there yet is peace betwixt us, and trifle no more."

"Dost thou not know," asked Robin, "of a certain curtal friar in these parts named Tuck?"

"Mayhap I do, and mayhap I do not. If thou meanest him of Fountains Abbey, the place is but a few rods down the glade when thou hast crossed the brook."

"Ay, truly," said Robin, "but I see no place to cross without wetting my new hosen. I pray thee, therefore, kind and good Friar, carry me across on thy broad shoulders. Come, tuck up thy robe and bend thy back that I may meet this same curtal friar in seemly fashion."

Then the Friar closed one eye, screwed up his mouth, and placed his finger upon his brow as in deep thought. At last he said: "What—if the good Saint Christopher were so willing, my unworthy self should not refuse." So saying, he laid down his missal and, tucking up his skirts, took Robin Hood on his back. He plunged into the flowing water up to his waist, carefully feeling his way over the pebbles on the bottom, and spake no word, good or bad, until he reached the further bank.

Then Robin leaped lightly from his back and set off briskly for Fountains Abbey.

"Hold! Not so fast, my fine fellow!" cried the Friar. "For

THE FRIAR TOOK ROBIN ON HIS BACK

ROBIN HOOD

now I bethink me I have left my missal and my steel cap upon the other side."

"Well," quoth Robin, "naught hinders thee to go back and get them."

"Nay, but," quoth the Friar, smiling, "one good turn deserves another, and therefore thou must e'en carry me back on thy shoulders, for peradventure, with another ducking I may take a chill or fall sick of divers pains and rheums."

"What if I should not?" quoth Robin.

"Then I will baste thy hide with thine own sword which I carried safely over and now hold."

Now Robin liked not the thought of playing pack-horse to this burly Friar. But he bethought him that the fellow spake truly enough concerning the sword, so he bent his back, with no very good grace. Straightway the Friar began to prod his heels into Robin's sides to make him go the faster, though in sooth he had to go slowly and carefully over the rough bottom with so weighty a burden. But he spake no word, and after much floundering and splashing they reached the bank in safety, where the Friar got his steel cap and his buckler.

"Now," quoth Robin, panting and sweating with his hard work, "it's my turn, and thou shalt carry me back, or I will put a shaft through thy fat body as easily as a maid skewers a capon."

"Why, so I will," quoth the Friar. "So put up thy bow, and come along, for it is ill to shoot upon a holy man that hath done thee a service."

So Robin once more mounted the broad back of the lusty Friar, and, becoming jubilant, shouted, "Come up, gee, woa!" rapping with his heels the stout Friar's shins, who quietly plodded along, without a word, toward the middle of the brook. But of a sudden he gave a mighty heave of his shoulders, and Robin flew right over his head into the brook with a loud splash, while the Friar stood holding his broad ribs from bursting with laughter.

"Now, my fine fellow," he cried, "choose thou whether thou wilt sink or swim!"

ROBIN HOOD

Robin Hood spake no word, for his nose and mouth were full of water, and he had no breath to spare. He swam to a bush of broom that overhung the bank and dragged himself ashore. Meanwhile the Friar leisurely waded out, shaking with mirth.

Robin, full wroth, met him with bow bent and arrow nocked to the string.

"Now, thou false Friar, thou shalt die," he cried, grimly.

But the other never blenched. Raising up his buckler he said:

"Shoot on, thou fine fellow. I tell thee if thou shootest here a summer's day, I will never flee thee."

Thereat Robin lowered his bow. "Nay," quoth he, "on second thought, I will not shoot thee dead where thou standest, rascally hedge priest though thou be'st. But with my good broadsword I will let thy blood. Therefore, arm thyself and make ready, for if I do not carve the brawn from off thy fat jowl, by Saint Dunstan, I'll supperless to bed for two moons."

"Be not so hasty," quoth the Friar, calmly. "I'm ready and willing as a maid is to wed." He slowly set his steel cap upon his head, and then, grasping his broadsword firmly in his great fist, he faced Robin with a bold front, bawling out: "Now, my crowing cockerel, I'll clip thy comb and spurs anon—yea, shake thy wet feathers!"

Thereupon they rushed together with a loud clash of steel and flying sparks, but ere long Robin saw that he must curb his hot blood or soon have it spilled; for the Friar, though angry, was calm and determined, bearing down Robin's guard with his heavy arm. So they fought from right to left, up and down, back and forth in the glade, with a savage fury and noise as if 'twere a whole company at fray.

Hour after hour the battle went on, with short pauses for rest, both panting and sweating, eying each other in silence, for neither had breath to waste in speech. From ten o'clock that morn had they struggled, and now past noon they were still tearing, slashing, and cutting with aching arms and tired backs; yet neither had a scratch.

"Hold!" bellowed the Friar. "Let us give o'er for a space

ROBIN HOOD

to take a midday bite and quench our thirst. Then, to it again."

"Not so, thou tough mountain of flesh," shouted bold Robin Hood. "Not till my sword hath taken toll on some part of thy body will I give o'er."

"Nay, hold thy hand but a moment, thou doughty fellow," quoth the Friar. "Wilt thou not suffer me to take off this hot steel cap to cool my brow? For the sweat poureth down in mine eyes to blind me."

"Yea, do so, but quickly," said Robin, the better pleased that now the broad shining poll would be a fair mark for his sword. Then the battle began afresh. Do all he could, Robin failed to strike the Friar's crown; and he in turn missed Robin a hundred times—and so the grim fight raged till four in the afternoon.

The ferns and woodland flowers were trodden into a shapeless mass among the soft, black loam. The song-birds had long flown away affrighted at the clashing din. At last bold Robin cried:

"A boon, a boon, thou curtal Friar! Give me leave to set my horn to my mouth, and to blow three blasts upon it."

"That will I," quoth the curtal Friar, lowering the point of his sword. "I care not for thy blast, though thou blow so passing well that both thine eyes fall out."

So Robin set his horn to his lips and blew three loud blasts. Scarce had the Friar heard the echo when he saw two tall archers with shafts ready nocked come running over the lea.

"Whose men are these," cried he, "that come so hastily at thy call?"

"These men are mine," said Robin Hood. "And what is that to thee?"

Then the curtal Friar saw that he had been tricked, but he abated no whit of his boldness.

"A boon, a boon," he cried, mimicking Robin, with a shrewd glint in his eye, "like to that I granted thee! Give me but leave to set my fist to my mouth and whistle thrice."

"That will I," quoth Robin, "for it is but just and fair. Three whistles from a Friar's fist will be a glad and blithesome sound, I trow."

So the Friar put his fist to his mouth and gave three loud whistles. The next moment there came half a dozen great mongrel dogs tearing along, barking loud as they drew nigh.

"Here, thou cowardly villain," said the Friar, "are a couple of shaggy hounds for each of thy men, and I myself will be enough for thee. At 'em, my pets, tear their green jerkins to shreds, my hearties."

Thereupon, two great, ugly mastiffs climbed in front and back of Robin in a trice before he had time to defend himself or flee. At last, torn and ragged, he got him to a tree and sat, with legs astride a stout limb, watching Little John shoot at the fierce brutes. Then he saw what made him doubt his eyes, for the dogs leaped aside from the flying arrows, caught them in their mouths, and broke them in twain.

"This is witchcraft," thought Robin, "and the Friar is a wizard, for never might dogs do so of their own nature." His wonder grew when he saw Will Scarlet step forth boldly toward the hounds with no weapon in his hand.

"Down, Beauty; down, Bess," cried Will, cuffing them right and left. Straightway the dogs began to cower down and fawn upon him, and gamboled about him as he stepped toward their master.

"What meaneth this?" quoth the Friar. "Have my dogs gone daft to love the company of thieves and cutthroats? Have I not, with their aid, kept Fountains Abbey seven long year and more from baron, knight, and squire, and must I now yield myself to three beggarly yeomen that dare to beard me in mine own dale? Tear them, tear their limbs asunder, good dogs!"

Will Scarlet now came forward, petting a great, ugly hound.

"Marry, stout Friar," quoth he, "cease thy brawling and curb thy wagging tongue."

"What!" said the Friar. "Do mine eyes behold young Will Gamwell in company with such a brace of deer-stealers? Now, I swear by holy Saint Boniface I will—"

ROBIN HOOD

"Peace, Friar, and hear!" cried Will.

Then, pointing to Robin, he said: "This stout yeoman who seemeth ill at ease perched in yonder tree is none other than my good uncle, Robin Hood. The other tall fellow is Little John, his good right-hand man; and hither they have come to bid thee join our merry band of outlaws in Sherwood Forest. Call off thy mongrel dogs and let us speak together and set matters right."

"Right well," quoth the Friar, "do I know Robin Hood by report, but doth he think to get me by cracking my bones? In troth, I ache and am full sore."

At length, somewhat appeased and soothed by Will's manner and words, he whistled off his hounds. Then Robin climbed down the tree and Little John with him drew nigh unto the Friar.

"For a holy man," quoth Robin, "truly thou art the stoutest fighter that e'er I clapped eyes upon."

"Nay, good Robin, thou art the better man, I trow, for never was I so weary of any man in fight." With that he pushed forth his brawny palm, saying, "Right glad am I to meet the bold outlaws of Sherwood Forest."

"And now," quoth Robin, "all being well, we will together go in search of Friar Tuck, whom we came seeking; and thou, holy Friar, must guide us."

"By my troth," laughed Will, "thou hast not far to seek, for that same holy friar now stands before thee."

"What?" exclaimed Robin. "Surely thou art not Friar Tuck!"

"The same," quoth the Friar, with a twinkle in his naughty, laughing eyes, "that gave thee a duck in yon stream."

"And the same," laughed merry Robin, "that drained the bottle of good Rhenish wine. Truly my mouth waters to think upon it. Hast thou no more of the like by the fountain? for after such sound buffets, given and ta'en, we would both, I trow, be the better for good meat and drink."

"Right gladly," quoth the Friar, "will I welcome you to my humble hermitage, though I fear me the fare is but a sorry crust. But come away all to my abbey, and mayhap with endeavor we may find enough."

ROBIN HOOD

Then all strode down the glade, and the Friar unlocked the stout door with a large key hanging from his belt.

"Welcome," quoth he, "to my poor lodging and its scanty fare."

They were ushered into a little room, entirely bare, except for a small, plain table and stool. "Tarry here while I make search for food and drink." So saying, the Friar disappeared for a time, and returned anon with a broad smile on his fat face. Silently he beckoned them to follow down a dark passage to another room. It was much larger and wider than the other, with a low ceiling, into which was let a large stained-glass window, which gave the only light. This window the Friar had carried away in pieces, earlier in life, when he had helped to build the beautiful priory at Coventry.

For you must know that in those early days only the churchmen were architects, artists, and writers. Many of the beautiful cathedrals, like Lichfield, were then a-building, and up to the present time nothing to equal them in church-building has been done.

Thus it was that the room had plenty of light; but nothing could be seen in it from the outside. In the corners were low couches covered with rich fabrics, and from the walls hung a number of images of the saints and a large, beautiful crucifix. But Robin and his men had eyes only for the table in the middle of the room, with four chairs ready set; for upon it were a big, uncut venison pie, large pots of honey, plenty of cakes, and many tankards and beakers of good ale and wine.

"This room," quoth Friar Tuck, with a merry twinkle, "is only used by mine own dear friends—the outer room serves for strangers. And now fall to, merry brothers, after a blessing, and let us see what we shall do."

They did as they were bid, doing full justice to the jolly Friar's bounteous fare. Amid the laughter and merriment Will told how he had joined the band; and, together with Robin and Little John, he begged Friar Tuck to become one of them.

"We are," quoth Little John, "much in need of a holy man, to christen and to marry, and oft to chasten us when we quarrel."

ROBIN HOOD

"Well," quoth Friar Tuck, "in truth, I like not well to change my quiet life to live among a band of outlaws. But it may be that it is my duty sithen ye say ye have no holy man among you. Nay, go to," quoth he, wagging his head, "methinks as a holy man I have no choice. What saith the good Saint Christopher touching the saving of sinners?"

At this Will Scarlet laughed loudly. "Nay, if thou comest, 'twill be because of thy most unholy love of hunting, quaffing, and good company. But make an end, sweet chuck, and say thou wilt come."

Then they all urged him right heartily, until at last he gave his word.

"Let us away," quoth Robin, "without more ado, for the hour groweth late."

"By the mass, not so fast!" said the Friar. "Tarry ye here and rest for the night with me. Then on the morrow early we will gather up all needful things for my comfort, and ye shall help convey them to Sherwood. Also my dogs must not be left behind, and I must lock up the Abbey snug and tight against the time we may need it."

To this Robin agreed, and after big draughts of nut-brown ale each lay down on a couch, tired but happy, for a good night's slumber. In five minutes all were fast asleep save Robin, who could scarce rest for his aching bones. Anon he heard a strange, rasping sound in the neighborhood of the Friar's couch, which grew louder and louder till it became such a deep roar as to make the room tremble.

"Holy Saint Withold!" thought Robin. "What is that horrid sound like unto a wild bull's roar? In truth, I cannot rest with such a din. Let me search, and mayhap I shall find the cause." So saying, he got up, moving toward the couch on which the Friar lay, to find the deep tones proceeding from Tuck's wide-open mouth. "So, it is thou!" quoth he, and gave the Friar a dig in the ribs, whereat the other did but give a loud grunt. But after more digs he at last raised himself sleepily, saying, "How now, good Robin? 'Tis not the morn as yet."

ROBIN HOOD

"Nay," quoth Robin. "Good faith, I wish it were. Thy snores grievously disturb my slumber, so thunderous and so awful that in sooth my spirit quakes. Canst thou not sleep where the din cannot reach me?"

"Lie down," said the Friar, "and I will keep awake till thou sleepest."

So Robin got to rest and waked no more till he heard loud shouts from the Friar, which told him that the morning meal was ready. Straightway they all arose and went to the fountain for a cold dash of water on their faces and a deep draught to drink.

The day was yet very early; 'twas scarce three o'clock. The purple haze and a yellow streak in the sky proclaimed the sun was up. The skylark soared aloft, its song fading in the distant clouds, and the woods resounded with joyous bird-notes. Full merrily they set to work, when their meal was ended, to help the Friar gather his belongings, while the dogs ran hither and thither, happy to be free. Slowly the Friar turned the key in the great lock. Then, with a wistful, last look at Fountains Abbey, he turned his face toward the forest, and with his companions silently strode forward on the road to Sherwood.

VIII

ROBIN MEETS TWO PRIESTS UPON THE WAY

JUST as the sun reached high noon the four travelers came forth from the forest trees into the glade of the great oak. A rousing cheer greeted Robin and his companions. They were well weighted down with things owned by the Friar, who was fain to bring all his gear and his weapons—his many bows, shields, and mail-coats, and great store of arrows. "For they are my dear friends," quoth he. The six mongrel dogs felt strange among so great a press of men, and were, as yet, in no humor to be petted or to make friends.

"I warrant them to be kind in a few days," quoth the Friar, as they snapped and snarled.

Quoth Robin to his men: "Have any of you heard aught of what goes on in the great world?"

"Yea," answered one. "Our spies in Nottingham town hear that King Henry hath died in his palace of Chinon in France of a broken heart, because of his sons, John and Richard, who, with the barons, joined the French King against their own father. Now Richard is soon to be crowned King of England, and after that, say they, he goeth upon a crusade to the Holy Land. All

ROBIN HOOD

the highways are thick with people on their way to London from York, Chester, and other big towns. The whole kingdom is sore distraught."

So Robin Hood bethought him that now would be a good time to enlarge their treasures—to give back to the poor what the rich and powerful had stolen. Straightway he and Little John laid their heads together. Small companies of the band, each under a leader chosen by Robin, were set to guard and watch certain roads and lanes nigh unto the forest. For the most part, the outlaws were disguised. As beggars, palmers, minstrels, or monks went they forth.

On a fair morn, as the warm, yellow sunlight trickled through the branching leaves, Robin boldly strode alone through the forest, bound for a certain bend of the great highway that a forest path joined. For while he dearly loved his companions— Little John most of all—it was his great delight to seek adventure alone. Many a hard knock had he gotten because of his hardihood, yet so sure was he of his own strength and skill that he hated the thought of help even from friends.

So, garbed as a friar with hood, gown, beads, and crucifix, and with his trusty sword hidden beneath his gown, he struck through the forest and came to the highroad. For once he had left his quarter-staff and long-bow behind. Anon he stopped to rest, and sat him down by the roadside upon a large fallen tree-trunk, mossy-green with age. Three happy, smiling maidens passed by with a "Good day, dear father," that brought forth in deep tones a solemn reply, "Benedicite!" At last he spied some distance down the road two lusty priests, clad all in black, riding comfortably upon the broad back of a strong, heavy-limbed horse. Going forth to meet them, Robin, with his hand on the horse's bridle, addressed them:

"Benedicite! Take pity on me, for our Dear Lady's sake. Nay, but one silver groat shall content me. For truly I have been a-wandering all this day and have gotten naught—not so much as one poor cup of drink nor bit of bread."

"I prithee, Friar, let go the bridle," quoth one of the priests,

ROBIN HOOD MEETS LITTLE JOHN

Page 36

THE BRIDE OF ALLAN-A-DALE

Page 94

ROBIN HOOD

"for by our Holy Dame, we have not a penny. Early this morning, hard by the forest, we were robbed of all we had by two bold varlets dressed like thee."

"Nay, by the mass," quoth Robin, "I fear me thou speakest false, for I am well acquainted with all the honest outlaws of Sherwood, and know full well that none but myself weareth hood and gown." At these words, catching a glimpse of a broadsword handle peeping through his robe, the priests began thumping the horse with their heels. But Robin picked up his gown round his waist, and with running soon overtook them.

"Now, by my faith, ye shall both come down in a trice," quoth he. Then, reaching up, he caught both their cowls and pulled them from their horse.

"O, spare us, Friar," cried the priests. "Thou wouldst not rob from the Church. Think of thy cloth, take pity, and have some remorse. No good can come of such a foul deed."

"Now, look ye," quoth jolly Robin, "if indeed ye have no silver, no harm shall befall you. For as much as ye said but now that ye had none, I am resolved that without more ado we all three shall fall down upon our knees and try whether we may get it by praying. So, down upon your knees and pray with all your hearts."

The priests looked up and down and all about them, but they saw naught save the blue sky, the green trees, and the white road. At last, perceiving that there was no help for it, they got them to their knees, and in right mournful tones besought the saints to aid them. "Send us, O send us silver to serve our need," they cried—then in a whisper, "that this bold, wicked villain may go his way and leave us in peace."

"Pray more earnestly," quoth Robin. "I fear me we shall get no great sum at this rate."

Then they began to wring their hands, calling upon the saints right lustily. Sometimes they wept, while Robin did merrily sing to cheer them on. But after a space he wearied of this sport.

"Now, by the mass," said he, "we will see what the good

saints have sent us, and will be sharers all alike of their bounty without deceit or guile."

Then the priests with doleful countenances put their hands into their pockets, but drew them out empty.

"Marry," quoth Robin, "ye have both prayed mightily, and it cannot be that ye have not been heard. Therefore, let us, one by one, search one another."

So first of all Robin searched the priests, and anon he poured out upon the grass a great store of gold—full five hundred pieces.

The two priests watched him with very sour faces and sorrowful hearts. "Alas," quoth one, "had we given him the groat he asked for, this grievous thing would not have befallen." Trembling, they waited on their knees to see what would be done with the money. At last quoth Robin:

"Here truly is a brave show—such a store of gold as does mine eyes good to look upon and maketh our hearts glad. I warrant neither of you looked for such a windfall. Sithen ye have prayed so heartily, ye shall each have a part. I shall give to each fifty pounds, and the rest I will keep for myself."

Both priests sighed wondrous deep, but never a word they spake. Rising from their knees, they moved away to mount their horse lest Robin should happen to change his mind and make them divide again, or perchance take away from them that which he had freely given. When they had taken but a few steps Robin said:

"Nay, tarry awhile. One thing more I have to say ere ye leave this place."

"What wouldst thou more?" they asked.

"Marry, this: ye shall make three vows that I shall tell you. The first is, that ye shall never again tell lies wheresoever ye go. And the second oath, that ye will be charitable to the poor and needy; and the third oath ye shall swear is to tell it abroad that ye met with a holy friar who taketh only from him that hath and giveth to him that hath not." With much groaning and murmuring and shaking of heads, they took the three vows. Then Robin set them on their horse; and away they went down the road at a

"PRAY MORE EARNESTLY," QUOTH ROBIN

sharp trot, glad indeed to have escaped without further harm.
Robin watched them, chuckling.

"Faith, Robin, thou hast done very well," he said to himself,
as he took a by-path toward the forest. "I would fain have had
thy service in this matter"—patting the hilt of his broadsword—
"but patience, good friend, we must bide our time." As he moved
leisurely along, thus communing with himself, he heard snatches
of a merry lay, accompanied by the notes of a harp, blending
together in sweet harmony.

"Truly," quoth he, "one who can trill such silvery notes must
surely carry a purse, wherein some golden coins may perchance
jingle another tune with my good aid."

So he stood behind a tree and listened as the singer came
toward him. The stranger was a tall young stripling with long,
golden, curly locks, and dressed in bright scarlet. He carried
the harp before him as he played, and seemed a happy and free
minstrel. "I will be sworn," thought Robin, "that yon tuneful
bird hath nothing to pluck save his scarlet hosen, and them,
forsooth, I want not; so let the light-hearted youth go by.
'Twere foul shame to break the tune."

As the singer passed on the music grew softer in the distance
and at last died away. Then, since the sun was near setting,
Robin set out for his woodland home, well content with the money
he had taken from the two priests.

IX

ALLAN-A-DALE GETS HIS BRIDE

HEN Friar Tuck heard Robin tell the tale of the two priests he laughed so heartily that he split asunder his leathern waistband, and, with tears trickling down his fat cheeks, quoth he: "Truly, Robin, thou art too kind and forgiving. Had I been there, the fifty pounds would never have rested again in their pouch."

"Nay, Friar," quoth Robin, "in that thou art wrong, for be it remembered we make it a rule to strip none bare, but to leave a crust even to a lying priest. What is more, they withstood me not, but obeyed like lambs led to the slaughter."

"Ay," said the Friar, "they well knew that to fight with such a one as thou would surely gain them naught but cracked crowns. Howbeit, I have it in my mind to join thee in the next adventure and take my part as may befit an outlaw friar." Then he sucked in his lips as if such a deed would taste as sweet as roast pig.

"Well," quoth Robin, "we will at once make ready—Little John, Will Scarlet, thou, and I."

Then Robin went to attire himself as a merry harper, with many-colored ribbons tied about him and with a gay plume of

ROBIN HOOD

feathers in his cap, his trusty broadsword and bow for weapons. Soon all four were striding through the forest.

They had gone scarce a mile when they espied a young man with head drooping who at every step fetched forth a sigh and oft wrung his hands, crying, "Alack, and well-a-day!"

"By my faith," quoth Robin, "I warrant this youth is none other than the same gaily dressed scarlet bird whom I heard but yester eve singing a roundelay in the forest. How comes it that he is changed so soon to a sniveling, ragged, ill-clothed varlet such as we now behold. Go thou, good nephew Will, and bring him to us, for verily I would know the reason of so strange a turn of fortune."

So Will Scarlet stepped forth toward the weeping, unhappy youth, who, upon seeing a man approach, nocked a shaft and bent his long-bow, crying, "Stand off, stand off! What is your will with me?"

"Naught that is harmful," quoth Will. "Our master, Robin Hood, whom thou seest standing beneath yon greenwood-tree, bids thee straightway go before him to answer certain questions he shall ask of thee."

At last the doleful youth laid by his long-bow and, going quietly, without demur, stood before bold Robin Hood, who spake him fair and courteously.

"How is this? Last eve I saw thee gaily dressed, blithesome, and jolly, singing like a happy cock robin to his mate, and now, behold, we find thee bedraggled and downcast. How may this be?"

Thereupon the youth drew himself up and looked upon Robin with a show of boldness.

"Nay, why should I tell thee this?" quoth he. "If thou meanest aught of ill to me, let me tell thee thou hast naught to do to harm so poor and wretched a man. Truly I have naught in the world save five shillings and a ring that I have kept these seven long years against the time of my marriage."

"Do but tell us thy woe," quoth Robin, "and mayhap it shall be well with thee."

ROBIN HOOD

Then the youth, seeing kindness in Robin's face, took courage and said:

"In sooth, I know not why thou askest, yet I will tell thee the whole matter, for it is all one to me whether thou meanest well or ill. Yesterday I was to wed a lovely maid, but she was torn away from me by her cruel father, who chose to make her marry a rich old knight. Wherefore my heart is slain, because I have neither money nor lands."

"Does the maid love thee, or hath she changed her mind of a sudden, as maids will?"

"In truth, she loveth me dearly, but they have torn us asunder, and will force her to be married this very day, and that is the cause of my unhappy state."

"Truly," quoth Tuck, "if she love thee, and be willing, why dost thou not take her away by main force? Thou wert ready enough but now to use thy bow upon us. Try the same trick upon the old knight. I'll warrant he will soon repent of his bargain."

"It is her father I fear," replied the youth, "and to him I would do no harm."

"Come, tell me," quoth Robin, "what is thy name?"

"By the faith of my body," said the sad fellow, "my name is Allan-a-Dale."

"Now what wouldst thou give," quoth Robin, "to one that would help thee to thy true love again and deliver her unto thee?"

"I have no money," quoth the tearful youth, "nor ready gold, nor fee, therefore mock me not."

"I mock thee not," said Robin, "but I have a mind to help thee."

"If thou dost the thing thou sayest," cried Allan, "right gladly will I swear upon a Book forevermore to be thy true servant and to do any deed for thee that is laid upon me."

"Well," said Robin, "tell me without guile, how many miles from here is the church where the wedding is to be?"

"In sooth, it is but five short miles, and by an easy path could I guide thee thither."

"WE FIND THEE BEDRAGGLED AND DOWNCAST"

ROBIN HOOD

"What say ye, my comrades, shall we help the poor lad to his true love?"

"Ay, that we will," chimed in the others, with one accord.

"But," quoth Little John, "we shall need help from our comrades. Do thou, Will Scarlet, go back to our trysting-place and choose twenty stout fellows to meet us at the church."

"Yea," quoth Robin, "and tarry not by the way. As for us, we will go with this youth to see how they make ready for the wedding."

So Will Scarlet strode off at a good gait, while Robin, Little John, and Friar Tuck started down a path toward the church, which they reached within an hour. They found no signs of a wedding, so they waited under a great yew-tree in the church-yard. Anon came Will Scarlet with his men, and Robin bade them keep hidden under the forest trees, but within sound of bugle-call.

Meanwhile, Friar Tuck had observed a priest trying to open the great church doors, and, stepping forth, he addressed him.

"Let me, aged brother, give aid to unlock the door."

"Grammercy, holy Friar, that will I gladly. Thy brawny hand is more fit to wield so large a key, and, I doubt not, hath handled a more dangerous weapon ere now."

"Nay, not so, pious priest. Thou seest before thee a most peaceful man, Friar Tuck of Fountains Abbey, most happy and content when at his beads and fasting. They tell me," he went on, "there is to be a wedding here this day."

"Ay, worthy Friar, and in brotherly love I will tell thee, from such an unfitting bond can come no good."

"Saist thou so? And why?" asked Tuck.

"The noble knight, good man though he be, is old enough to be the maiden's grandfather—a gaunt, rickety bag-o'-bones with one leg in the grave—and the poor, pretty maid stark crazy in love with a more fitting mate. But her father, misguided man, for money will force her to it, and vows she shall marry the knight willy-nilly."

"Here they come," quoth Tuck. "The cavalcade now rides

[89]

ROBIN HOOD

up the road. Canst thou not, good priest, hide me that I may witness the wedding in the church?"

"In truth, I can. Go behind yon stone column in the little chapel, where thou wilt hear and see all."

The wedding procession was slowly coming up the road toward the church. In front rode the knight, Sir Hugo de Ferrico, with the Bishop of Hereford on one side and on the other the Prior of Emmet. The knight, on a gray charger, with his sallow, gaunt face between the jolly, fat, red faces of his companions, looked like a honeysuckle between two peonies. Then came the maid's father, a sour-looking Saxon franklin; and behind him rode the daughter, a beautiful maid on a white palfrey. Behind her, again, rode the wedding guests, four of the knight's men-at-arms, and the attendants of the churchmen.

When Robin saw the haughty churchmen dismount from their horses, he borrowed Allan-a-Dale's harp, then strode boldly up to the church door and began to thrum and sing.

"What," quoth the fat Bishop, "do we have sweet music to welcome the wedding guests?" Then, eying Robin closely, he said, "What art thou, and what doest thou here dressed so gaily in bright ribbons and feathers?"

"I am a bold harper, the best in the north country," said Robin. "Men say the strains of my music do make the heart glad, and the newly wedded to love each other forevermore. Many a happy bridegroom hath crossed my palm with golden coins, from the river Dee to Trent, from Derwent to Avon."

"Ah, truly," said the Bishop, "then do thou at once show us thy skill while the fair bride dismounts to enter the holy church."

"Nay, by the mass," quoth Robin, "that is against my rule." For, to say sooth, he could not play a tune to save his life. "I always play a march while the wedding guests walk up the aisle, and softly soothe the harp to silence as the ceremony begins."

"I vow," quoth the Prior, "the harper is right, and a very pretty thing 'twill be."

Thus it was that Robin waited till all had entered. He closely watched the rickety old knight hobble up in an effort to hand the fair maid from her palfrey, and he thought he never before had seen a face so sweet and gentle as hers. Pale and sad, she looked about like a frightened fawn, seeming to hope that even at that late hour some good saint would intervene and save her from the vow that would bind her to this old dotard of trembling limbs.

When all had entered, and the Bishop was ready to march with stately strides up to the chancel, he turned sharply round upon Robin, saying, "Now tune thy harp and make music, thou lazy rogue, for see, the bride moves toward the altar."

"Marry, that I will not, till I see thee with the Book."

"Thou saucy, beribboned varlet, I will have thee flogged when all is done." So saying, the Bishop took his place and opened the Book to marry. Robin then boldly marched up and placed himself between the bride and the groom.

"By holy Saint Dunstan," he loudly cried, "this is no fit match. Thou art too old and shaky, Sir Knight, to wed a maid so young and tender. The bride shall choose and wed her own dear love that is of her own age and sound of heart and limb."

Then all the company stared in silent surprise at Robin, who put his horn to his mouth and blew three loud blasts that made the rafters ring. Straightway the knight reached for his sword— but he had forgotten it when putting on his wedding clothes. He shouted to his men-at-arms: "Slay this bold varlet that dares disturb the rites of Holy Church."

But as they were about to lay hands on Robin, who had no weapon, but stood ready with the harp to defend himself, running up the church came twenty archers clad in Lincoln green, led by Little John, Allan-a-Dale, and Friar Tuck.

Allan thrust Robin's trusty long-bow into his hands, and as he took it the maid's father said to him, in angry tones:

"Thou art a knavish hind to bring this trouble on us now."

"Nay, say not so! I, Robin Hood, and my stout archers, have come hither to right a woeful wrong and see two fond lovers united."

"It shall not be," quoth the father, "unless thou first slay me."

ROBIN HOOD

At the name of Robin Hood all the people stood aghast, the men-at-arms shrank back, and the knight turned in stately silence away. Robin boldly stood his ground, holding his trusty bow, with Little John and the others at his side. A solemn stillness reigned in the church; the Bishop and the Prior held each other up in trembling fear, saying to themselves, "May the saints protect us from this naughty villain and his wicked green-clad hinds." Then they tottered toward the door, but Robin shouted:

"Stop, holy churchmen, I have use for you ere you depart, and mean you no harm."

Then Sir Hugo, the knight, spake in pride to the maiden's father.

"Had I known thy fair daughter loved and was beloved of another, by the mass, I would not have wished her to share my castle, my lands, and my proud title. Take thy daughter and give her to the poor minstrel if so be she loveth poverty better than riches." Then with his men-at-arms he hobbled down to the church door, mounted his horse, and rode away.

"Be this as it may," the father cried out, "she shall never marry a poor starveling, who, I'll warrant, hath not a groat to patch a torn doublet."

"In that I vow thou art wrong," quoth Robin. "Give him the bag of gold, Little John, that I took the other day from the lying priests."

Then the bag of three hundred golden coins was emptied out to appease the angry father. At sight of them his face changed.

"Is all this money thine, Allan-a-Dale?" quoth he.

"Nay," quoth Robin, "it is thine, an ye give us thy blessing on the wedding now to be, though she shall be wedded, blessing or no, for we doubt, coming from so sour a father, if it be of any avail."

The heap of gold was tempting, and the old franklin bethought him that since Sir Hugo had taken himself off he would not easily find another rich suitor. So at last he said, sighing deeply, "If my daughter must e'en marry Allan-a-Dale, why, good faith,

ROBIN HOOD

marry him she shall." Then all the wedding party cheered and were glad at heart.

"Now," quoth Robin, "my Lord Bishop, we do but wait upon thee to join this loving couple without more ado. So get thee to thy place and open thy Book."

"Nay, thou saucy varlet," said the Bishop, with flashing eye, "this may not be. The banns have not been read in church three times o'er, as thou shouldst know is the law of the land and of Holy Church."

"Then cry the banns thyself, Lord Bishop, to marry these two lovers whose plighted troth needs but thy good help."

"Nay, by the mass, that will I not," shouted the Bishop.

"Then, an thou wilt not," quoth Robin, laughing, "I will make mine own bishop. Stand forth, Friar Tuck, and put on the bishop's robes."

With that Robin pulled off the Bishop's coat, then took off the Prior's gown for Little John. All the people howled with laughter to see Friar Tuck tricked out in such fine array. The faces of the Bishop and the Prior were purple with anger and shame, but they dared not stir a finger.

"If thou art ready, Little John, step up and take thy place to cry in church this loving couple three times aloud, that Friar Tuck may wed them."

Then Little John went up into the choir, whereat the people began to titter. But he was no whit put out of countenance, and he cried the banns seven times o'er lest three times should not be enough.

When he had finished, Robin called him down, and to see him walk with head up and chest pushed out, so like the Bishop, sent a merry peal of laughter through the church. But the laughter swelled into a very roar, as Friar Tuck, with a wink of his mischievous eye, took the Book. With a show of spirit the Bishop cried in fiery tones, pointing to the gorgeously attired Friar: "This man is no true priest. 'Tis but a rascally hedge priest."

"What saist thou, proud Bishop?" bellowed forth Tuck, his

[93]

ROBIN HOOD

body shaking with rage; and, dropping the Book, he rushed toward the Bishop like an angry bull at a red coat. "No priest, quoth-a! I stand here before thee as much a priest as thou art, a holy clerk in orders, the Vicar of Fountains Abbey, a pious, holy man that loveth his neighbors, that doth not rob the poor to cover his back with fine clothes, nor line his belly with good food. Go to, proud churchman, and be thankful that I am a man of peace and that my quarter-staff is at mine abbey, or it would soon play a tune upon thy gross body."

His choler somewhat abated by so long a speech, he turned, puffing and blowing, again to take up the Book, which he calmly, half smilingly, opened, and in a loud, husky voice began to read. At last came the question, "Who gives this maid to wed?"

Quoth Robin Hood: "That do I, and he that takes her from Allan-a-Dale shall buy her full dearly."

Then the ring was placed on the finger of the blushing, happy bride, whose face, heretofore so pale and wan, was now like a blooming, rosy peach. The wedding was over and the noisy, happy crowd pushed forward to speak fair words to the wedded lovers. Then Robin said:

"Take off the churchmen's robes, and give them back, for, in truth, we have no further need of them. Here, Prior, is thy robe, and we thank thee for thy holy presence; and, Bishop, here is thy coat. But, stop, that gold chain round thy neck is unbecoming to a holy man, and more seemly for the pretty throat of our queenly bride."

The Bishop made a wry face and turned to go.

"Give it up," roared Robin, "or I will tear it from thy fat neck in a trice."

Meekly the Bishop obeyed, and Robin gracefully wound the massive golden chain round the neck of Allan's bride. So then the Bishop and the Prior trotted down the church at a merry pace, glad indeed to get away with their skins whole.

"Thus," said Robin, "having ended this merry wedding, we will now go hence to our happy glade among the leaves so green."

So they hied them back to Sherwood Forest, where they feasted

ALLAN·A·DALE

ROBIN HOOD

and pledged the bride in flagons of foaming ale. Allan sang for them until his voice grew hoarse.

If you remember, Allan had promised Robin that he would be his servant forevermore. So the outlaws built a bower for him and his bride, who dwelt thereafter in the forest with Robin and his men. And for many a long year Allan-a-Dale's tuneful songs shortened the weary hours in foul weather and made the sunshine seem brighter. At their feasts or their sports he never once refused a song, and sometimes of a moonlight summer night he would leave his happy bower for a while, then softly go to where the outlaws lay sleeping on their leafy, open-air beds to sing a love song or lullaby of ancient days. Or perchance he would rise very early before the dawn and awaken them with a morning hymn. Thus he entwined himself in the hearts of them all.

X

HOW ROBIN HOOD DID CHEAT THE TINKER

YOU must know that the Bishop of Hereford and Prior Emmet as they rode away from the little church were in a towering passion and spake many harsh words of the merry outlaws, but more especially of Robin Hood.

"The shameless, thieving rogue!" said the Bishop, dolefully. "The bold, naughty villain, to tear off my chain, every link of which is solid gold, that would exchange for six tuns of good wine! But I'll have it back," quoth he. "I'll have it back, for I'll set the Sheriff's men to scour the woods and make these same outlaws skip away like rats, that we may be rid of such vermin."

"We ought to thank the saints," quoth the Prior, "that the saucy varlet took no more."

"Good faith, holy father, what more could he have ta'en from us save the coats from our backs or the skin from our bodies?"

"Thou wottest not," answered the Prior, "that my pouch contained fivescore golden coins, and I do wonder his sharp eye noted it not when first we met. But so soon as I saw what was toward

ROBIN HOOD

I hid the pouch in the folds of my robe, that he might not be tempted to give the maid a dower. So shouldst thou have done with thy golden chain, my Lord Bishop."

"The chain is too costly for the child of a Saxon hind to keep," grumbled the Bishop. "Natheless, the villain spake with a semblance of truth when he said such gauds do ill become a holy churchman."

Thus they talked, sadly enough, as they rode toward Nottingham town. The Sheriff received them with such courtesy as their high state in the Church demanded; but as the tale of the wedding was unfolded he grew paler, and his body shrank together, till at last, when he heard of the golden chain, he threw up his hands in despair, crying:

"Alack, alack-a-day! will my whole life be ruined? Is there no end? Will troubles never come singly? The barons rob the Jews, the outlaws rob the Church—what is to become of our unhappy land? For I need an army to cope with such fell deeds. The King's foresters will not go near this hornets' nest, for fear of being stung with their arrows. My men-at-arms start and grow pale at the very name of Robin Hood. Indeed, I myself dare speak his name but in a whisper for fear the wretch may at any moment rise from the very floor of my house like an evil spirit. Day or night, sleeping or waking, the name haunts me so that I am like to go daft. Do thou, good Bishop, cudgel thy brain to find some remedy, for mine own groweth soft and watery."

"All I can advise," said the Bishop, "is to draw up a warrant in the King's name, and to publish broadcast that a great reward is offered for the outlaw's capture. Surely there are many strolling, hardy villains outside Nottingham who, for a round sum, will attempt to rid our land of this pest. I myself will give a hundred pounds to get my chain again, and do thou, Sheriff, offer another hundred. Such a noble sum will doubtless draw many brave hearts to the adventure."

So it was soon noised about in Nottingham town that a great reward had been offered to any who should capture the bold

ROBIN HOOD

outlaw, Robin Hood. Messengers on horseback carried the news north and south. A notice was posted upon the door of the Town Hall, but the townsfolk only laughed. They knew it was no hard matter to offer a reward, but not so easy to earn it. Indeed, they were sure no single man would be found foolish enough to try.

It so happened one day that a number of men were seated on a bench, drinking ale at the door of the Blue Boar Inn, round the corner from the Town Hall, in a narrow street hard by the Convent of St. Andrews. The talk ran upon the warrant, and the most interested listener was a burly, ragged tinker, with turned-up nose, rough, shaggy face and hair, and dirty leathern apron. Traveling from town to town all over the country, he earned but little with mending of pots and pans, and what little he earned was soon exchanged for ale and beer.

"What do I hear," quoth he, "two hundred pounds to catch a thief? Dick o' Banbury, thou hast been tinker long enough; a thief-catcher is a better trade. No more kettles to mend for me! If my crab-tree staff doth not crack a hole in this rogue of an outlaw's pate, then I am no man of metal. For now my motto is to crack instead of to mend."

So he hied him to the Town Hall door, where he found the proclamation posted.

"Truly," quoth he, "I am no scholar, and must e'en search for one that can read and expound the substance."

As he stood there scratching his head a cowled monk stepped up to him.

"What wouldst thou here, my son?" asked he.

"Fain would I read what is here written, but I cannot."

"That is easily mended," quoth the monk, "for I will read it to thee."

After carefully listening and nodding his approval at each item, Dick the tinker started off at full speed to the Sheriff's house. The steward came forth angrily at the loud crack of Dick's staff on the door. Before the tinker could find his tongue the steward said, gruffly:

ROBIN HOOD

"Go thy way. We have no pots and kettles that want mending in this place."

"Look you, fellow, I mend no pots, but I would ask the Sheriff to give me the King's warrant to catch that vile outlaw, Robin Hood."

"Truly, good tinker, that's a cat of another color. Step in, brave tinker, bold tinker"—then, to himself—"fool tinker, thou art in the way of trouble."

Dick o' Banbury was the first to come seeking the warrant, and you may well believe the Sheriff was right glad to receive him. "Ay," thought he, looking Dick up and down, "he's lusty, and looketh bold, but is he sly?"

"Well, my brave lad," he said, aloud, "so thou seekest to win our reward?"

"Ay, marry, that I do, my Lord Sheriff. If the saucy deer-thief be still alive I shall nab him with the help of this, my good crab-tree staff."

"I warrant he's alive," quoth the Sheriff. "Thou lookest bold and strong withal, but art thou sly?"

"Ay, that I be," said Dick, "slyer than a fox. Was ever a weasel caught asleep, was ever a dog seen to run from a meaty bone, or a cat from a sparrow, or a mouse to leave a bit of cheese? So surely am I sly!"

"Well, tinker, here is the warrant," said the Sheriff. "And now thou hast it, see that thou dost act as boldly as thou speakest. Catch this fellow, snare him, trap him, beat him, or kill him, I care not. If thou dost bring him to me dead or alive, thou shalt surely have the reward and we will attach thee to our service at good wage, to boot."

Then, calling the steward to give Dick a foaming tankard of good ale, he hurried him off on his quest. The ale put the bold tinker in fine fettle, so that as he strode along he twirled his staff round his head so fast that the passers-by blinked and stood aloof.

But, being full of vainglory and pride because he held the King's warrant, he could not refrain from stopping once again at the

ROBIN HOOD

Blue Boar Inn. He had no money to wet his whistle; yet, though talking was dry work, he wished to make it known to all that he, the man of metal from Banbury, would show these north-country folk how to crack pates.

Just as he had sat him down a fine fellow, dressed all in red with a long sword at his side, came up and stood anigh him. Straightway Dick's tongue began to wag.

"Good sir," quoth he, "if thou dwellest in these parts, mayhap thou hast heard of a varlet named Robin Hood."

"Surely," quoth the man in red, "thou art a stranger that asketh this. All men hereabout do know Robin Hood, by report, for a rascally, bold outlaw. But what is thy name and whence comest thou?"

"I am from the south, and Dick the Tinker o' Banbury am I called. Having cracked all the noddles in those parts, I have come hither, by the mass, to crack more."

"I thought thy trade was to mend, not to crack," quoth the stranger. "I have doleful news for thee."

"Marry, I warrant thou canst say naught that would grieve me."

" 'Tis that two of thy tinker brethren were set in stocks for getting drunk on ale."

"I care naught for thy gibes," snarled Dick. "There be no true tinkers but could drink all day, and still be sober. I'll warrant thou durst not try me."

"Well," said the stranger, laughing, "now that my news is stale, what is thy news? For in thy gadabout life thou hast surely gathered some moss of that kind. Perchance a tankard of ale will grease thy throat and make the news run more smoothly."

"Ay, that it will. Well," said Dick, after a deep draught, wiping his grizzly beard on the dirty sleeve of his doublet, "I will tell thee a thing to make thee marvel. Thou seest me, a poor man—a mender of pots and pans, forsooth—yet I tell thee I am about to pick up two hundred pounds without even stooping—in faith, as easily as a rabbit slips down his warren."

ROBIN HOOD

"By St. Withold, saist thou so? Come, out with it; let's hear of so marvelous a trick."

"Why," quoth Dick, " 'tis no great matter, if a man be bold and strong and cunning withal. Marry, 'tis this: I hold the King's warrant to seize that naughty thief and outlaw rogue, Robin Hood. An I clap eyes upon him, I'll Robin him. I'll singe his red breast, and make him whistle another tune. Somewhere near by in this forest he lies. Can'st thou not guide me to where this fox hath a hole? Do so, and I'll give thee some part of the reward—a vast sum, truly—two hundred pounds, and the Sheriff's dear love, to boot. Nay, by the mass, I can feel the gold coins clink in my pouch already. Hast ever seen the villain?"

"Ay, marry, that I have," replied the stranger.

"And what is he like?" asked Dick.

"In truth, he is of about my size; folk say we are as like as two peas from a pod."

"Bah!" quoth the tinker. "I thought he was a very bearded giant. An he be like thee, I vow to bind up one arm, and cudgel him with t'other."

"Yet they tell me," was the reply, "that he swings a quarter-staff right smartly, and hath some skill with the sword. In good sooth, tinker, he carries a long-bow full seven feet long— but let me see thy warrant to know if it be right."

"That I will not," the tinker said, "for none will I trust with it."

"But drink, brave tinker, thou art not afraid of the stocks."

"How can I drink from an empty mug?"

"Thou saist truly," quoth the stranger. "Bide here awhile, and I will ask mine host to tap a certain brew of foaming Ut-toxeter ale, that I wot of." With that he slipped inside the tap-room and told the host to mix some strong liquor in the ale, which he then took out to the tinker.

"Marry," quoth Dick, "that is the right ale for stout hearts."

"Drink up, spare it not, there is more on tap," cried the stranger, just sipping a little to keep company. "Ay, empty again! Good mine host, fill up the tankard with that right good liquor. The tinker likes it well."

By the time the next cup was finished, the tinker waxed so jolly that he began to sing snatches of a merry ditty of the southland. Then, gradually becoming quieter, his eyes closed, his head nodded to one side, and in a twinkling he was fast asleep, snoring loudly. Thereupon the stranger rose silently from his seat. With a smile on his face he reached over, unbuttoned the tinker's pouch, and drew forth the warrant. Then on tiptoe he stole into the Blue Boar Inn and paid the host his score.

"But wake not the tinker," quoth he, "till I be out of call."

In a little while mine host bethought him that it ill became his well-kept house to have a dirty-looking tinker fast asleep at his front door, so he stepped outside and shook him roughly.

"No more," yawned Dick, "my jolly blade. We had enow; I am content, good comrade."

With another hearty shake, mine host angrily replied:

"Nay, do not comrade me, thou drunken rogue. Get thee gone."

The tinker, now half awake, opened his eyes and saw the fat landlord of the Blue Boar Inn. "Where, what, how, why am I here?" he muttered. "And where is that scarlet fellow that was here but now? Methought he would lead me to that bold thief, Robin Hood."

"That jolly blade with whom thou didst drink," said mine host, "was none other than Robin Hood himself."

"What saist thou—Robin Hood—for whom I hold in this very wallet a warrant!"

Then looking down, he saw that the pouch was open and the warrant gone. Straightway he leaped up and stared about him wildly. He thrust his hand into his pouch and drew it forth empty. He looked in his bag of tools, under the table, under the chair. Then, taking up his staff and swinging it above his head, he roared:

"My warrant hath been stolen from me while I slept, and thou, pig-faced villain, doubtless watched that sly red fox take

WITH A SMILE ON HIS FACE HE REACHED OVER AND
DREW FORTH THE WARRANT

ROBIN HOOD

the King's warrant from my very body. Thou scurvy hog, I will beat thy back till it be as blue as the boar on thy swinging sign."

"Pay thy score or I will have thee put in the stocks as a drunken knave."

This answer brought the tinker to a quieter mood. "Did not the naughty thief pay for me?" he asked.

"No, not a farthing, he!" said mine host.

"Alack-a-day!" quoth Dick, with a rueful face. "Not a farthing have I. Oh, could I but meet him now, I would square the score with both him and thee!"

"Thou wilt best do that by leaving here thy bag o' tools and thy quarter-staff."

"Nay, good landlord, without tools and staff I can neither work nor fight. Let be the staff, that I may have wherewith to beat the thief to jelly, if by good hap I meet him, and so get the reward to pay thy score."

"Very good," said mine host, somewhat softened. "Bring me back ten shillings, and thou shalt have thy bag of tools again."

"But," quoth Dick, "in sooth I know not which way to turn to catch this wily thief."

"The only way," said mine host, "is to seek him among the parks, where thou mayest find him killing the King's deer."

So the tinker departed from the Blue Boar Inn with a sore heart and downcast mien. But soon he grew more cheerful. "I care not for the warrant," he muttered, "could I but see him once again," and he strode on at a quicker pace, ever and anon playing his crab-tree staff right merrily as though Robin even then stood before him. After an hour or more he had wandered aimlessly some distance along a forest path and had made up his mind to a leafy bed in the forest that night.

"Patience, good Dick!" he said to himself, "and on the morrow thou shalt belabor this knave!"

Scarce had he spoken when he saw a red-coated fellow approaching through the leafy glade. "Holy Saint Swithin!" he whispered. "I vow 'tis the pretty Robin redbreast, as sure as a

ROBIN HOOD

cuckoo steals eggs. May that good saint clip his wings that he fly not nor escape me. An he be nimble, so am I. He comes nearer. Shall I hide? Nay, I'll go forward and meet him; if the villain run, I'll run faster."

They were now but a few paces apart. So far, Robin had not noticed the tinker, but looking up he caught his angry glare full upon him. So furious, indeed, was Dick that he stood speechless in front of Robin, who calmly said:

"What knave is this that doth come so near my path in the forest?"

"Knave or no knave, thou scurvy red villain, my crab-tree staff shall show which of us hath wronged the other."

Then like lightning did the tinker whirl his quarter-staff so near that Robin barely had time to draw his sword and save his head. Dick the tinker was in a tearing rage, for he had more than one count to settle—first, to gain the reward; second, to get revenge for the stealing of his warrant; third, to punish Robin for the loss of his tools of trade and forced payment of the score at the Blue Boar Inn.

In truth, he was an ill fellow to meet in fight, for he was taller and bigger of bone than Robin. He had a bullet-head set upon a bull neck, from which big blue veins bulged out with exercise and fiery passion. Moreover, what with long practice in every town he visited and brawls with every sort of men, his quarter-staff play was of the best. As for Robin, he had but his broadsword—a weapon unsuited to parry the heavy two-handed strokes of the mighty tinker.

Never in his life did Robin flinch or give way to any man he met, but now he found that he had thought too lightly of the tinker's strength and skill. Thus it was that from the beginning he was forced to defend himself very shrewdly. Dick's powerful staff, seven feet long, with great ugly knots at each end, was played with wonderful nimbleness, and soon he gave Robin a fearful crack that half stunned him and made him reel forward.

Then Robin put forth his utmost strength, clashing his broadsword against the staff so that the splinters flew, guarding many a

THE TOWNSPEOPLE PAY TITHES TO THE HOLY CHURCH

Page 156

THE BISHOP OF HEREFORD ROBBED IN SHERWOOD FOREST

Page 161

ROBIN HOOD

blow and rapidly flashing his sword so close to the tinker's head that he seemed every moment to miss it only by a hair. The blade was of finely tempered steel, and it neither snapped nor showed a dent. Oft the edge would have carved a sore wound but that the tinker's staff was handled with wondrous deftness. The furious encounter went on for some time in silence, save for the sound of wood beating upon steel and the heavy panting and grunts of the foemen. The outlaw seemed to gain slightly, pushing his more burly antagonist backward, though the crab-tree staff whirled around as before. The tinker was very hard pressed, and almost fit to flee, yet he fought right manfully, and at last with a sudden turn he brought the heavy cudgel down in a swift and cruel blow that fell upon Robin's arm and numbed it so that his fingers lacked strength to grasp the hilt. Then the sword dropped to the ground.

"A boon, a boon," Robin cried. "Do but grant me a boon!"

"Not I," quoth the tinker. "Before I do I'll hang thee on this tree." Then, tired as he was, he began to dance about in high glee, shouting in a merry voice, "The reward is now mine own, for the outlaw rogue is under my thumb."

As for Robin, he spake no word, but he set his bugle to his lips and blew three loud blasts.

"How now!" growled the tinker. "I like not thy music, so come with me straightway, or I'll sauce thy goose with my cudgel again." So saying, he pointed his staff unpleasantly close to Robin's head.

At that moment three men came running at full speed toward the spot.

"What is the matter, Robin," quoth Little John, "that thou sittest so sore astonied and sad-looking on the highway side?"

"Matter enow," said Robin. "There stands a tough rogue with his quarter-staff that hath belabored my hide and made it full sore. I warrant he hath broken my arm, so much it paineth me."

"Good faith," quoth Little John, "I fain would try if he'll do so much for me." Gripping his quarter-staff by the middle, he

ROBIN HOOD

wrathfully approached the tinker, who backed against a tree and roared:

"Come on, thou daddy-long-legs. I'll tie thy spindle-shanks in a Staffordshire knot and serve thee as I served thy master."

Their quarter-staffs had scarcely crossed when Robin cried out: "Hold, good comrade! The man had good cause to beat me so. I took from him the warrant for my arrest with which he hoped to mend his poor estate. Come forth, tinker, I am too sore as yet to move. I love to have brave and handy men in my band, and thou art both, meseems. But, tinker, remember the odds are now against thee. Our holy Friar, my cousin Will Scarlet, and my right-hand man, Little John, all three hunger to beat thee to jelly. Yet I would now have peace. Without the reward, what is thy lot?"

"In sooth," quoth Dick, "a sad one. Without tools I cannot work to redeem them."

"Look you, then," said Robin. "I would have thee join our band in merry Sherwood. A fair share in all we take shalt thou have—plenty of venison to eat, good ale to drink, a suit of Lincoln green, and a hundred pounds to boot. What saist thou—wilt thou join us?"

"Marry, that I will, right gladly," quoth the tinker, joyfully. "A bold outlaw's life will suit me well, and I will ever be thy true servant."

So Dick the Tinker o' Banbury joined the band, and you will hereafter see how well he played his part among the merry, brave outlaws in Sherwood Forest.

XI

LITTLE JOHN AND THE SHERIFF'S COOK

ROBIN'S arm was broken, indeed, so that for weeks he had to have it bandaged and keep it in a sling. But the tinker, who grieved sorely that he had caused this hurt, bound it up and dressed it right skilfully. For you must know he had himself been wounded so oft that there were few men who knew more of broken bones or bruises. So from that time forth he was often called upon to act as bone-setter or leech. It was Dick's peculiar pride to show the wondrous number of dents and holes in his pate. Indeed, he always spoke of his head as "my pepper caster." In less than a week every outlaw in the band had felt for these same holes and dents through Dick's shaggy hair, and much they marveled at his pluck and the thickness of his skull.

Nearly always, when Robin Hood gained a stout fellow for his band, he got a sound beating at the same time, but he never changed his brave demeanor nor ceased to try each man in hand-to-hand fight to prove his worthiness to join the company of gallant outlaws. All must be bold and brave like himself, so that when a final test should come each should be found true as steel. But in shooting with the long-bow Robin excelled

ROBIN HOOD

them all, and was never beaten either in accuracy or distance. Thus till the day of his death all his men loved him for himself and nigh worshiped him for his skill with the bow.

At this period of England's greatness, the bowmen were most feared on the field of battle. Many famous warriors were shot to death by arrows. At the battle of Hastings, King Harold was shot through the eye, and many others fell pierced by shafts from the long-bow. The second Norman King, William Rufus, was shot through the heart with an arrow while hunting in the New Forest. Even the lion-hearted King Richard himself, after so many hand-to-hand fights, was slain at last by an arrow shot by a young French archer.

And as the bow was the greatest of weapons, so Robin was known far and wide as the greatest of archers. Never was there another like him either before or after his time. He was not only a brave captain, but a wise one; and he looked well to the comfort of his men, that they might have good store of food and clothing. Each and every one was called upon to do his share in providing for their daily needs. Those who were deft in making arrows and bows had their duties. In forging or mending steel weapons each took a part. Others had to bake, roast, and boil the victuals for so large a company. Their food was mostly venison, game, and wild fowl, fish in plenty from the rivers, and oaten, rye, or wheaten cakes. Wild berries, fruit, and nuts, and wild honey eked out their supply. On such wholesome fare did the outlaws thrive, and as each season advanced a goodly supply was stored.

During the cold, dark, stormy days of winter they kept them to their caves and snug retreats, sitting round the blazing logs for warmth and light as darkness fell. They wiled away the long evenings with never-ending tales of love and war; of ancient sagas and legends, interspersed with the ever-welcome harp notes and songs of Allan-a-Dale, their minstrel. In such fashion the days passed quickly and merrily by. It was now nutting-time, and the yellow leaves had begun to fall; but Robin still kept him to his bower nursing his wounded arm. Outside Sherwood

ROBIN HOOD

Forest, Nottingham town was busily astir with its great annual feast and October fair. The great King Richard had taken a mighty army of nearly all the young men in the country on his crusade to fight the Turks in the Holy Land. But Robin cared little enough in his pleasant forest retreat for wars or the doings of kings and armies.

On a day, when the merry men had returned from gathering great skin bags full of hazel, beech, and chestnuts for roasting at the winter's fire, Little John came to the bower to beg his master's leave to see the fair. Thereat Robin considered for a space and seemed right loath. At last he said:

"Yea, go, if thou hast such a stomach for the adventure; but see that thy disguise be good, for the loss of my right-hand man would be a sore hurt to me and all our band."

"Marry, I will go clad as a sturdy, tattered beggar with a crooked shoulder and a limp of one leg."

So Little John cast off his well-fitting suit of Lincoln green and donned such a rag-tag jumble of clothes that the merry men roared with laughter when they beheld him. Then, with sword at his side and bow slung across his shoulders, he strode off through the forest in high spirits toward Nottingham Fair.

The fair brought always a vast throng of idlers and merry-makers to the town. Since it lasted a week, or rather from Monday to Saturday night, there was need of many shows, games, trials of skill, and wonders of all sorts to entertain the great throng that poured in from all over the country, even from the far-away towns of Derby, Lincoln, and York.

Little John passed down the long line of booths, gaily decked with buntings, where ribbons, gewgaws, and such things as women and children love were sold. Then he sauntered to a part of the fair where only men and boys seemed to gather. Here a raised stand had been set up with a wooden railing about twenty feet square. Its rough, wooden floor had been sprinkled over with a good supply of fine white sand. Here were held public contests in boxing, wrestling, and quarter-staff play; and here among the laughing, noisy crowd stood bold Little John

ROBIN HOOD

in his beggar disguise, watching intently a famous wielder of the quarter-staff, Eric o' Lincoln, who was cracking the pates of any and all the Nottingham lads who dared try their hands and risk their heads against this champion from Lincoln town.

Eric was one of those who visited fairs and such like gatherings in different towns to fight with quarter-staff for prizes and wagers. He was a tall, well-made fellow with broad shoulders and sinewy arms. His knotted muscles, through constant exercise with a heavy staff, were of unusual size, and he was right vain of them. He had just toppled over on the boards, with little effort, two brawny Staffordshire fellows from Stoke and Trentham, and now stood bolt upright holding his staff in front of him, shouting in a defiant voice: "Marry, come up, my lads! The day is not far spent, yet I tarry too long for a bout. Are all the brave lads dead, or are one and all afeard to meet Eric o' Lincoln?"

The bustling crowd fell silent for a space, staring at one another, but none ventured to mount the stand. Still Eric urged them to come on, even with promises of a prize could they withstand him for but a brief space. At last Little John could contain himself no longer. He turned to the crowd, saying, "Will any lad lend me a stout staff to try a bout with this crowing braggart?"

Such a speech from a ragged, crooked beggar raised a laugh. Nevertheless, many held out their weapons. Little John quietly looked them over, and chose the one used by the man from Stoke, a wicked-looking staff of hickory, heavy and long, neatly crossed with hide thongs to make the hand-grasp less slippery. Still pretending a bent and crooked form, he climbed up the steps and placed himself in a fighting attitude on the stand facing stout Eric, who said, loud enough for all to hear:

"To think I be forced to cross my staff with a saucy beggar! I vow to befriend him with a few pennies when he is carried off the stand with a cracked noddle."

"Peace, thou chattering cockatoo, and defend thyself!" quoth Little John sternly; and, falling to right merrily, he deftly rapped

HE SMOTE ERIC FULL AND SQUARE ON HIS SKULL

ROBIN HOOD

Eric a stiff blow upon the shoulder, which made the crowd stare and then laugh.

Eric eyed the beggar more closely and noticed that his broad shoulders began to straighten up to a height even greater than his own. Then began the battle in good earnest, each man feeling that he had met a worthy foe. The blows fell thick and fast, so that time and again the men in the crowd caught their breath, thinking that one or the other of the combatants must surely fall. But every stroke was stoutly met and parried. Quoth one, "Never was such play seen before in this town." Another asked, "Who can this tall lad be?"

Meanwhile, the fight continued with no advantage on either side. The beggar now seemed a very giant that with crashing blows time after time made Eric's staff tremble. The temper of the crowd had changed. It was all for the beggar now, and encouraged him with ringing cheers and promises of plenty of money and good things should he win this famous bout.

At last, amid a din of yelling jeers and groans, Eric crashed a heavy blow on John's broad chest, but as the blow fell so did John bring his staff down on Eric's skull with a resounding whack that was heard by all the throng. Another shout went up, then all fell silent.

Before John could strike another blow Eric had gotten over the stupor caused by the stroke. He ducked, then ran back while John's staff crashed on the floor with a terrific bang. The staff was a good one, and held sound, else Little John would then have bit the sandy floor, so savagely did Eric now run upon him. Careless of his guard, in a fury of madness, Eric put forth all his strength and skill, and for a few minutes the air was filled with cracking blows that none but a tower of strength like John could have withstood for a moment. But he stood there on guard, calm and crafty, waiting an opening for a final blow, which he well knew from such careless, angry fighting would sooner or later come.

In quarter-staff battles a loss of temper was fatal. Both fighters knew that a cool, watchful guard was the only way to

ROBIN HOOD

victory. But Eric understood by now that, in truth, it was no beggar who opposed him, and his anger swept away his prudence. That Little John bided his time so coolly but enraged him the more. For some minutes his fearful, crashing blows fell without a break or pause. Many and many a time did John just escape an ugly stroke that would have laid him low. But he steadily parried and feinted until at last his time came. Then with a quick, downward, heavy swing of both ponderous arms he smote Eric full and square on his skull, so that his body dropped, limp, with a thud upon the sandy floor.

Instantly from the quiet, hard-breathing crowd came a volley of deafening cheers. The battle had lasted fully two hours and had drawn nearly every man from all parts of the fair. Many now crowded round Little John with offers of money and other good things as he gave back the staff to the man who had loaned it and had held his long-bow while he fought. Then, tired and thirsty, John and the man from Stoke together strode away, and were soon lost in the press of people. They made their way to the Blue Boar Inn to refresh themselves, it being now somewhat past the hour of noon.

"Thou art no beggar," quoth the sharp-eyed man from Stoke, "and dost go in such guise for some purpose of thine own. Tell me, brave comrade, thy name, for if thou canst use thy long-bow with half the skill wherewith thou didst wield my staff, the archery prize is thine to take this afternoon."

"What saist thou?" quoth John. "Is there a shooting-match this afternoon?"

"Ay, that there be," said his companion. "The Sheriff offers a prize, and we will together go and try for it."

"Marry, that we will," quoth Little John.

So now together they strode toward the shooting-butts, where they found the archers ready to begin. Then, entering their names as competitors, they made ready for the shooting. The place was crowded with a great mass of men and women, all eager to catch a glimpse of those who were about to shoot, for in those days every skilled archer was known far and wide, so

ERIC · O' LINCOLN

ROBIN HOOD

that as each man took his place folk told each other what prizes he had won and what feats he had performed. Foremost in the crowd were those who had witnessed the quarter-staff bouts earlier in the day, and a shout went up as they recognized the man who had overcome stout Eric o' Lincoln.

"Ho for the mighty beggar!" they cried. "Now for some good sport. Now, Sir Tatters, thou dost surely deserve a prize." Such words were sweet music to the ear of Little John, though he showed it not, but waited patiently his turn.

Marvelous shots were made—so keen indeed was the rivalry that the beggar's admirers cooled somewhat toward him. Were not the cream of the best archers competing, drawn forth from three surrounding counties—men whose equals could scarce be found in merry England!"

"Now, rag-bag, 'tis thy turn," quoth Adam Caverswall, who up to now had beaten all the rest. "Canst thou mend that shot?"

"Maybe, and maybe not," quietly replied Little John.

Two targets had been set up, and between them a wand stood upright holding a small wreath of flowers. Adam had planted a shaft in the center of each target, and thought that he would surely win. So thought the crowd who, fickle as the wind, now cheered him instead of the beggar. Chuckling slyly to himself, but saying not a word, Little John nocked his shaft so slowly and deliberately that both the other archers and the people waxed impatient, for they longed to see what he would do.

"Wake up, beggar," quoth one. "Bestir thyself, and let us see if thou canst hit the mark."

But no reply came from Little John's smiling lips while his bow bent farther out, till the point of the cloth-yard shaft nigh touched his thumb. Then he loosed the string with a twang. Hastily fitting another arrow, he shot again, and still once more—three shots, one after another, without a pause. Then the expectant crowd gave vent to a mighty roar. "A champion, a champion!" they cried. "The ragged beggar shoots more true than Robin Hood." For the first arrow had sped through the middle

ROBIN HOOD

of the floral wreath, and each of the others had cut one of Adam's shafts from the target.

As for the Sheriff, he swore a deep oath. "This man," quoth he, "is the best archer that ever I saw. Not even that bold knave Robin Hood could best him, and right well hath he upheld the honor of the town in quarter-staff play."

Then Little John stood in the presence of the proud Sheriff, who thus addressed him:

"Tell me now, strong young man, what is thy name, and in what town wert thou born?"

Little John replied, "In Holderness was I born, and when I am at home men call me Reynard Greenleaf."

"Look you, Reynard, 'tis foul shame to see so young and brave a man in rags a-begging alms. I need full sore stout hearts about me. Wilt thou enter my service? Besides proper attire and a full stomach, every year I will give twenty marks to thy fee."

Then Little John thought awhile, and at last he smiled. "Your worship," quoth he, "I have a master, a courteous knight. Before I may enter thy service, noble Sheriff, I must e'en get leave of him."

To this the Sheriff agreed, and he promised that should Little John get leave to serve him for a twelvemonth he would make a present to the knight of a good strong horse.

So Little John went away and bided for a day, after which he came back and told the Sheriff that all was arranged. He took the horse and rode away to a little cottage in which dwelt a spy who knew the outlaws' trysting-place. Setting him upon the horse, he bade him ride away to Robin Hood, to give him this message: that Little John had entered the service of the Sheriff, and that for the short time he was there he would make the worst servant the Sheriff ever had. As for the horse, Robin was to keep it for himself. Little John returned to the Sheriff's house, where he was given a fine new suit of clothes and was made acquainted with the butler, the cook, and other members of the household.

On the following day the Sheriff started out early to go hunting;

ROBIN HOOD

and Little John, being very tired, overslept himself, lying in his bed till long past the noon-hour. At last he got up and dressed, then marched down to the pantry, crying out:

"Good Sir Steward, I pray thee give me to dine. Too long hath Greenleaf fasted, therefore prithee bestir thyself."

The surly steward was in a sour mood and liked not to serve dinners at odd hours.

"Thou shalt never eat till my lord be come to town," he said, gruffly.

"I make it my vow, thou saucy rogue, to crack thy crown unless both meat and drink be set before me straightway."

The fat steward strode back and forth in anger, then rushed for the buttery and shut fast the door; but with a running kick Little John smashed it open. It flew back with a thunderous bang, and the steward was sent flying over a barrel of ale. Then Little John forced him to drink so much that if he lived a hundred winters he would never forget having refused a meal to Reynard Greenleaf. Straightway the outlaw sat him down and made a hearty meal of all the good things in the buttery, not forgetting a full share of ale and wine.

While he sat feasting at his ease, the steward stole out through the door and hurried to the cook in the kitchen to tell him what had befallen. This cook was both stout and bold, and, though he had little love for the steward, yet he liked not that a saucy rogue should lord it where he was wont to rule. So he strode off to the buttery in a fiery rage, meaning to teach the new servant a lesson in manners.

"I make my vow," quoth the cook, when he found Little John still eating, "thou art a shrewd knave. What! Thinkest thou to eat when thou listest, and beat whom thou wilt? I will show thee who is master here." So saying, he let fly three good buffets which made Little John's ears ring and sent flying across the buttery a jellied chicken's wing, which he had just raised to his lips.

Little John slowly rose from his feast, saying, "In sooth, thou art bold, thou art hardy; but before I make another stride from

ROBIN HOOD

this spot I hope to settle two debts I owe thee. Thy cooking I like pretty well, and thy cuffs a little more. Now draw thy sword, for I mean to baste thy body with hot gravy."

The cook was not slow to obey, for he was no man to flee, and in truth he loved fighting better than feasting. Together they parried, slashed, and cut for over an hour, yet neither harmed the other.

"By my faith," quoth bold John, "thou art one of the best swordsmen that ever yet I saw. If thou canst shoot as well with a bow, to the greenwood I fain would have thee go, to join Robin Hood and his merry outlaws. I could get thee twenty golden marks every year for thy fee, two changes of clothing, and all the venison and foaming ale a reasonable body could wish."

At that the cook lowered his sword, and his eyes grew round as saucers.

"Who art thou that dost say this?" he cried. "Art thou, Reynard Greenleaf, one of Robin Hood's merry men?"

"Ay, that I am. Little John am I, and none other."

"Put up thy sword," cried the cook, "for I will no longer fight with thee. Bless the good-fortune that brought us twain together, for there is naught in all the world for which my heart so longeth as to be one of Robin Hood's merry men. And art thou in good sooth the famous Little John?"

"Yea, and right glad would I be to resume the meal thou didst so lovingly interrupt."

So they began to eat and drink together in the friendliest fashion. When they had stuffed themselves as full as they could hold, they strode off to the Sheriff's treasure-house, but found it locked and barred. Then the cook said:

"Tarry awhile, and I will go and get a heavy hammer from the kitchen." He soon returned and smashed in the door. After helping themselves to a number of silver vessels, cups, and other table silver, they opened a drawer and emptied therefrom three hundred pounds in money. Placing all together in two bags, they left the house, making straight for the forest.

ROBIN HOOD

They soon arrived at the glade, and both were made welcome by Robin Hood.

"Tell me, good John," quoth he, "what tidings dost thou bring from Nottingham town?"

"God save thee, my dear master," quoth Little John. "The proud Sheriff greeteth thee full lovingly and sendeth thee his cook and a-many of his silver vessels, with three hundred pounds in good money."

"Nay, by the mass," said Robin Hood, "I warrant it was never by his good-will so much kindness is done to me." Then the cook told what had befallen, and they all roared with laughter.

Little John then bethought him of a merry conceit. So off he started through the forest to a certain place where he thought he would find the proud Sheriff hunting with hounds and horn.

When he saw the Sheriff he knelt down before him and said:

"God save thee, my master dear."

"Reynard Greenleaf!" cried the Sheriff, in great surprise. "What hast thou now for me?"

"I have been in the forest," said John, "and I saw the fairest sight that mine eyes ever beheld. In yonder glade I saw a right fair hart, his color being of green, and by his side were seven-score deer, all ranged in a circle. The antlers of this hart had over sixty points, so sharp that I durst not shoot for fear it would slay me."

"I make my vow," said the Sheriff, "that marvelous sight I fain would see."

"Come with me, dear master, and I will show it thee."

The Sheriff gladly rode after the nimble, fleet-footed outlaw, and after a long trot they came to the glade and stood before Robin Hood. Then said Little John:

"Behold, there stands the master hart in the green coat."

The proud Sheriff stood still, and with a sorry face and sad voice replied: "Reynard Greenleaf, thou hast betrayed me. Thou art well named, for the fox is sly in the woods."

"In truth, master," said Little John, "thou art to blame, for I was refused a good dinner when I was a servant at thy house.

ROBIN HOOD

So now I will return good for evil and send you home with a good dinner."

In a very short time the feast was spread, and all the food was served upon silver vessels. When the Sheriff took up the cup of wine he looked very closely at it, then at the silver plate, and then at Little John. He could not eat for very sorrow when he found that the meal was spread upon his own silver.

"Make good cheer, for charity's sake," said Robin. "I warrant, Sir Sheriff, the fare is good. So eat and be merry. For the love I bear thy servant, Reynard Greenleaf, we will spare thy life and do no harm to thee, so fall to and prove thyself a good trencherman."

But the Sheriff was too sad; all he could do was to watch in silence while the others ate heartily.

When the evening began to close and the time came when all should go to rest Robin commanded John to draw off the Sheriff's hose and shoes, his cape of fine furs, and cap with plumes. John gave him a green mantle to wrap his body in, that the cold night dew might not give him a chill, and told off a number of young men to lie beside him on the greensward under the great oak.

But the Sheriff, used to soft living, lay awake all night long, shivering with cold, till his ribs began to smart and grow stiff. At last the long night was over and the dawn appeared. One by one the outlaws awakened and arose. Robin then asked the Sheriff:

"How didst thou fare in our way of sleeping?"

"A hard and miserable bed," replied the Sheriff, "and for all the gold in merry England I would not dwell in such a state."

"Nay," quoth Robin, "thou shalt dwell with me, I vow, a full twelvemonth, for I fain would teach thee to be a merry outlaw."

Quoth the Sheriff: "Were I to spend such another night I would rather that thou shouldst smite off my head, and would forgive thee for it. Let me go for sweet charity, and I will afterward be thy best friend."

"Then we will let thee go," said Robin, "but before thou art gone thou shalt swear to me a great oath on my bright sword—

ROBIN HOOD

that thou wilt never more strive to harm me, and that if thou findest any one of my men by night or by day thou wilt help him as well as thou mayest."

The Sheriff was so wretched that he promised everything and took the oath. Then Little John put him on his horse and, leading him through the greenwood a little way, parted from him with hearty good wishes for a safe return home.

XII

ROBIN TRIES HIS HAND SELLING MEATS

ROBIN HOOD was a little piqued at the crafty means by which Little John had gotten the better of the Sheriff. By the name he chose —Reynard Greenleaf, which means "fox from the woods"—he seemed to boast of his own slyness; and while Robin owned that his right-hand man was craftier than he had thought, he resolved that he would not be outdone, but would himself show the Sheriff a thing or two. He and his band had no hatred against the Sheriff, nor, for that matter, against any one else, much cause as they had to be bitter against the world, for they were all outlawed men. What they did was done in a spirit of jovial frolic and fun. It is certain that they never did any foul misdeed. They robbed the rich, who robbed others, that they might live and have means to help the poor and needy. In those cruel old days, when might seemed to make right, few were so kind and honest as Robin Hood and his merry men. Robin himself often went to mass at the little church on the outskirts of the forest, where he was welcomed because of his many lavish gifts. For he loved the humble and sincere churchmen even as he hated the purse-proud and selfish.

ROBIN HOOD

It fell upon a day that Robin started off alone through the forest singing a blithesome song. He had not gone far when he chanced to meet a jolly butcher, who likewise was singing merrily as he rode through the wood among the leaves so green. The butcher bestrode a fine mare, and swinging from behind on each side hung two great silk bags full of the meat he was taking to Nottingham market to sell.

"Good morrow, my fine fellow," quoth jolly Robin. "Tell me what goods thou hast in thy panniers, for I have a mind for thy company and would fain know thy trade and where thou dost dwell."

"Truly, a butcher am I, and to Nottingham do I go to sell my meats. But what is it to thee where I do dwell? Tell me thy name."

"My name is Robin Hood, and in Sherwood do I dwell."

Then in a trembling voice the butcher said: "I cry your mercy, good Robin, for I fear that name. Have mercy on me and mine; let me go my way."

"Nay, jolly butcher," quoth Robin, "fear nothing, for I will do thee no harm. Come, tell me, what is the price of thy meat and of thy mare, for, by the mass, be it never so dear, I fain would be a butcher."

"I will soon tell thee," quoth the butcher. Then he looked straight before him and for a space seemed lost in thought. At last he said: "Good Robin, I like thee well and would not offend thee. Therefore thou shalt have my meats, and eke my bonny mare, for four marks, though the price be beggarly."

"Get down from thy horse," quoth Robin, "and come, count out the money from my bag. Right gladly do I pay thy price, for I long to be a butcher for a day, and I warrant I shall sell my wares first of them all at the market."

When the butcher had seen the money counted aright he snugly packed it away in a little bag in his pouch, well content with his bargain; and Robin, mounting the horse, jogged off to Nottingham market. First of all, he got from the officers of the guild a market-stand, for which he paid a small fee. Then

ROBIN HOOD

he put on the butcher's apron, cap, and jacket, cleaned off the stand, got out all the legs and shoulders of mutton and veal, sharpened his knives, and was soon busy with cleaver and saw, cutting up pieces to make the best display in the market. All the other butchers looked askance at Robin because he was a stranger and seemed ignorant of the ways and sly tricks of the trade. However, when all was set out to the best advantage, he began to cry out in a loud voice:

"Come hither, good people, come and buy, buy, buy. I sell good meat cheap, and cheap meat good. Pay no heed to the other butchers, for they sell naught but bone and skin. Be not backward, good wives, good maids, good widows, and good spinsters; come up, come up and buy. I sell as much meat for one penny as you will get from the other butchers for three pennies. I will cut away all the fat and sell you the lean. An it please you, good dames, I will strip away all the bones and sell naught but flesh. As for the bones, ye shall take them home to your dogs. Six pounds of good fresh meat, with never a bone, for one penny!"

So lustily did Robin cry his wares that soon a throng of dames and lasses pressed about his stand, while scarce a soul came near the booths of the other butchers. Ere long his trade was so brisk that he had no need to shout. Then, when a pretty lass asked the price of a piece of meat, he would answer: "Naught, but one kiss from thy pretty lips." Thus the handsome young butcher got many a kiss, which gladdened him more than silver coins. Long before the market closed Robin was clean sold out, and the others were full wroth because they had not thriven that day. They talked with one another, saying, "Surely he is some prodigal, that hath sold his father's land and now wastes the money in selling meat at so low a price." Said one: "Perhaps he is a man of much store and cattle. We had best be friendly with him." So several of them stepped up to Robin, saying, "Come, brother, we be all of one trade, and the Butchers' Guild is to dine with the Sheriff. Wilt thou join us in the feast?"

"NAY," QUOTH ROBIN, "FEAR NOTHING, FOR I WILL
DO THEE NO HARM"

ROBIN HOOD

"Ay, marry, that will I," quoth merry Robin. "I will go with my true brethren, as fast as I can hie."

So they all marched off together to the Sheriff's house. The Sheriff had been told of this wonderful butcher who could afford to sell as much meat for a penny as the others did for three pennies, so he made up his mind to place Robin beside him as the honored guest, thinking to lure the young spendthrift into some bad bargain. When they had all sat down to eat, he asked Robin to say grace. Then Robin stood up, but he could think of naught to say. At last he muttered:

"Pray God bless us all within this place and eke our meat. A cup of good sack will nourish our blood—and so I do end my grace."

Then they all fell to and enjoyed the feast full well.

"Come, brother butchers," quoth jolly Robin, "while we do stay, let us be merry. Come, pour us more wine. I vow to pay the reckoning if it cost me five pounds ere I go. The cost is mine, so be merry, good friends, be merry."

While the butchers were drinking at Robin's expense they smiled and nudged one another and talked in whispers. "This is a mad blade," said one of them; "a wise one saves, and a fool spends." The Sheriff whispered to his left-hand neighbor, "His father hath left him lands which he hath sold for silver and gold, and now means to be rid of its cares." Then he said to himself, " 'Twere a good deed to help him in so worthy a purpose."

"Good fellow," quoth he to Robin, "hast thou any horned beasts to sell unto me?"

"Yea, good master Sheriff, that I have—some two hundred, as well as a hundred acres of good land, an it please you to see it. And I will make as good a bargain of it to you as my father did make to me."

"What is the price thou askest, my good fellow, for the two hundred horned beasts? For if the price be within reason, I warrant I shall find one who will buy."

"The price to thee, noble Sheriff, shall be small enough. 'Tis but two hundred pounds."

ROBIN HOOD

"Ay," thought the Sheriff, "but one quarter of their true worth. I must go to see these same horned beasts before it chance he change his price. By my faith, good fellow," he said aloud, "I fain would look upon thy two hundred horned beasts."

"That is easily done," quoth Robin, "for they are not far to seek."

So when the feast was ended the Sheriff had his palfrey saddled, put two hundred pounds in gold in his pouch, and made ready to go with the spendthrift butcher. Robin saddled his mare, and away they rode to the forest of merry Sherwood.

As they were passing through the leafy woods the Sheriff crossed himself, saying, "God save us this day from that naughty varlet, Robin Hood!"

"Amen, so be it," said jolly Robin, who was leading deeper and deeper into the forest.

When they had gone a little farther, bold Robin chanced to spy a hundred head of good red deer that came tripping along full nigh their path. "Look you," quoth he, "how like you my horned beasts, good master Sheriff? Are they not fat and fair to see?"

Then the Sheriff was wroth and fearful. He trembled in his boots, for a sad thought of a sudden flashed through his brain. Quoth he, "I tell you, good fellow, I would I were gone from this forest, for I like not thy company nor thy fat beasts."

"Tarry but a moment, Sir Sheriff," quoth Robin, and, putting his horn to his mouth, he blew three blasts, whereat Little John and all his company came running.

"What is thy will, my good master?" cried Little John.

"I have brought hither," laughed jolly Robin, "the Sheriff of Nottingham this day to dine with thee."

"Then, by Saint Swithin, he is right welcome to me, and I hope he will honestly pay for the feast, for I know he has gold. I can smell it in his pouch, and I warrant if it be well counted there will be enough to serve us with wine to drink a whole year."

Then Little John lovingly grasped the Sheriff round the waist and drew him down from his palfrey. Taking his mantle gently

ROBIN HOOD

from his back, he laid it on the ground. The proud Sheriff stood still and doleful while Robin opened his pouch and jingled out the two hundred pounds in golden coins into the mantle. Little John carefully picked up the golden pieces and deftly cast the cloak again upon the Sheriff's back, then set him upon his dapple-gray palfrey, saying, "Adieu, good Sheriff, I wish thee a safe journey home."

Robin took the bridle-rein and led the palfrey to the edge of the forest, where he bade the Sheriff God-speed.

"Commend me to your lady wife at home," quoth he, "and tell her that Robin Hood found much profit in the butcher's trade in fair Nottingham town this day." So Robin went away laughing to his bower.

XIII

ROBIN HOOD AND ARTHUR THE TANNER

OU will perhaps remember how Little John gave Eric o' Lincoln a mighty crack at Nottingham Fair, and how Eric went back home with a very sad heart and a sore head. He had purposely made the journey to meet and fight another famous wielder of the quarter-staff— Arthur-a-Bland, the jolly tanner of Nottingham. At that time Arthur was away at the wars in the Holy Land fighting against the Turks with King Richard. He had now returned with a large body of archers, while his King had been treacherously captured and imprisoned in a castle.

Now when Arthur came home he found the tanning trade— along with others—in very evil state; and, though for a time he was treated and toasted at every tavern in the town as a brave English archer who had seen the Holy Sepulcher, all this naturally came to an end, and his wonderful tales grew a trifle stale. Thus it was that Arthur became lonesome and pined for something to do.

During the hot midsummer days he was sorely tempted to enter into the cooling shade of Sherwood Forest and try his hand with the long-bow on some fat hart. The great autumn fair was

LITTLE JOHN GREETS SIR RICHARD O' THE LEA

Page 212

THE MEN OF SHERWOOD KNEEL TO KING RICHARD

Page 244

months away, so he could make no use of his quarter-staff, for it would do him no good to crack the pate of some passing stranger while he dwelt in the town. One fine morning very early he made up his mind to take the risk of killing a fine buck, so he girded on his sword, and, with his long-bow swinging at his back and stout cudgel in hand, he started off, twirling his staff round his head to the tune of a jolly roundelay. It was his first venture into the woodland glade since he had come home from the wars, and the quiet, cool peacefulness of the forest made him glad that he was no longer in the hot, sandy deserts of the East. The birds sang a blithesome tune, as he thought, in response to his merry song, so that soon he forgot all about sheriff's men, or King's foresters, and gave himself up wholly to his joy in the pleasant day.

Arthur was a shrewd, bold fellow, who would hold his own in any fight so long as he did not meet more than one foe at a time. His great cudgel was a thing to beware of. Nevertheless, as he strode deeper and deeper into the forest he became silent and glanced about him watchfully, not only in case of meeting a stranger, but to keep from frighting the deer.

Anon his sharp eye made out the antlers of a fine young buck coming toward him with a herd of deer. Crouching down among the ferns, he crept along till within fair shooting distance and nocked a shaft. He had not observed behind a tree a stranger dressed in Lincoln green who, like himself, carried a quarter-staff and bow. Just as Arthur tightened the string to let the arrow fly, the stranger in a loud voice cried out:

"Hold, thou thieving rogue and villain! Who art thou that rangest so boldly here? In sooth, thou lookest like a thief that comes to steal our King's deer."

In blank surprise Arthur turned round to view the bold stranger who dared accost him thus, and on seeing a single man no taller or stouter than himself, he replied:

"Nay, by the mass, what lying rogue art thou to call me a thief and a villain when I am neither any more than art thou? Marry, what is it to thee what I do?"

Then the stranger said: "I am the keeper of this forest, and the

ROBIN HOOD

King hath put me in charge of his deer; therefore I do hinder thee from shooting at them."

"If thou art a keeper in this forest," quoth Arthur, boldly, "and hast such a great charge, thou must needs have some help of others before thou canst hinder me, for thou art not of thyself able to do it."

"Truly," replied the stranger, "I have none here to help me to make thee stand, nor have I need of any, but I have here a good oaken staff that I know full well will do the deed."

"Thou green grasshopper," yelled the angry tanner, "I care not a straw for thy staff, thy sword, nor thy bow. If I but once rap thy bare noddle, thou wilt be put in bed well covered with sticking-plaster."

"Speak less boastingly," said jolly Robin, "and use better terms to me, or I will e'en mend thy manners without more words."

So saying, he unbuckled his belt, laid down his long-bow, and then, being aware that the tanner was making ready with his staff, he said:

"If thou dost choose to fight with staff rather than sword, so let it be. But before we begin our fray let us measure staffs, for if mine should prove the longer thou wilt count it foul play."

"I pass not for length," bold Arthur replied. "My staff is of oak—eight feet and a half. It will knock down a calf, and I hope it will knock down thee."

Then Robin rushed upon him and gave him such a wicked knock that the blood gushed forth from the side of his head. For the first half-hour the fight was a fierce staff-cracking tattoo. From the way in which Arthur ran around nimbly and laid on and parried, Robin saw from the first that he would have enough to do to defend himself. They were both running like wild boars, and both were bleeding from head wounds. The woods resounded with their lusty knocks, as each strove full sore to reach the other's leg, arm, or any part of his body. For two hours they plied their staffs with heavy strokes as if they were cleaving wood. Both were grimly silent, watching each other carefully for an opening that would end the strife. Arthur had met his

"MY FREEDOM HAVE I WON THROUGH MY STAFF,
AND NOT BY GRACE OF THEE"

ROBIN HOOD

match—much greater obstinacy and skill than he ever had met before or now looked for in his foe. He had not the least idea whom he was fighting, but he swore to master this bold fellow, whoever he might be, who dared to question his freedom in the forest. As for Robin, he remembered all too well the beating the tinker had bestowed upon him, and fain would he show Little John and his men that he could gain the mastery with some other weapon than the long-bow.

Another half-hour of the ceaseless din and clatter, and both combatants were a sorry sight, their faces covered with blood and sweat, both utterly tired out and aching with their wounds. "Hold thy hand, fellow," quoth Robin, "and let thy quarrel fall. Though we crack our bones all to pieces, we gain no prize, nor any other good thing, thereby. Hereafter in this forest of merry Sherwood thou shalt be free to do thy will."

This speech somewhat nettled the fiery tanner, who replied: "God-a-mercy for naught. My freedom have I won through my staff, and not by grace of thee."

"Prithee tell me, good fellow," quoth Robin, "what trade thou art of and in what place thou dost dwell, for I would fain know both these things."

Bold Arthur replied: "A tanner am I, and in Nottingham town have I long plied my trade. Shouldst thou ever go there, I make a vow, I will tan thy hide for naught."

"God-a-mercy, good fellow," said jolly Robin; "since thou art so kind, I will do as much for thee. My name is Robin Hood, and in sooth if thou'lt forsake thy tanner's trade to live in the greenwood with me, thou mayest shoot the deer and eat venison to thy fill—besides gold and fee, a fair share of all we take."

"I vow," quoth Arthur, "if thou be'st indeed the outlaw Robin Hood—and by the bruises of my body I doubt it not at all—then here is my hand in loving kindness. My name is Arthur-a-Bland, and we two will never be parted."

Robin gladly grasped the strong palm, happy in having stood up so long against a champion known far and wide as the boldest and deftest hand that ever plied a quarter-staff.

ROBIN HOOD

"But tell me," said Arthur, "oh, tell me, where is my dear kinsman, brave Little John, whom I've not seen for many a year? On my mother's side we are related, and I fain would set eyes upon him once more."

"He is ever," said Robin, "within sound of my bugle-call." Then he blew full loud and shrill, and scarcely had the echo died away in the distance when Little John appeared, running as fast as his long legs could carry him through the forest glade.

"Oh, what is the matter?" cried Little John. "And why dost thou, my master, sit there so sad and befouled? I fear me that all is not well with thee."

"Oh, my comrade," quoth Robin, "this tanner did make me stand, but he tanned my hide so soundly that now perforce I must sit. He is a brave blade and a master tanner, too. That I should know, having tasted of his trade."

"He is to be commended," quoth Little John, "for so great a feat, but if he be so smart at his trade, let him try to tan my hide, too."

"Nay, nay, stay thy hand," said Robin, "for he tells me that he is of thine own blood, and his name is Arthur-a-Bland."

Then Little John threw away his staff as far as he could fling it. Running up to Arthur, he put his great arms around his neck, and both did weep for very joy. When they had drawn apart, Arthur swore a great oath that hereafter, as long as he lived, the three should be as one; and, all joining hands, they danced round the oak tree, singing:

"For three merry men, and three merry men,
    And three merry men we be."

XIV

ROBIN AND THE BISHOP OF HEREFORD

I T is not likely that even such hard-headed fighters as Friar Tuck, the Tinker, and the Tanner had more dents and holes in their pates than had Robin. But he, brave and big-hearted, looked upon such matters as part and parcel of an outlaw's life. Of like dispositions were all his merry men, and they obeyed and followed him willingly. The life they had chosen, from either choice or necessity, was more enjoyable than any other they could find—yet they were not held against their wills. They could leave at any time if another and better path could be found. So they loved and trusted one another, and there was never the least chance that any would take aught from the secret store of treasures without the captain's leave, for all had enough.

The treasure was kept in a place so strong that the band could defend it against an army without being dislodged except by famine. After going through the trap-door of the great oak you emerged from a tunnel inside the massive walls into a court-yard, at each end of which was a square tower, built directly in front on either side of the cave-opening. This cave, being used

ROBIN HOOD

only for winter sleeping, was lighted and warmed by great log-fires. The side towers, built of solid blocks of stone, had each three large chambers, one above the other, reached by a winding staircase. The north tower was the armory, in the lower chamber of which suits of chain armor, knives, daggers, swords, bucklers, bows and arrows, and other weapons were plentifully stored. Above it was the clothiery, where great piles of cloth of every color and material were kept on shelves, together with many suits of clothes, both for disguise and general use. At the very top was the treasury, of which Little John and Will Scarlet had charge. In this chamber were heavy, iron-bound boxes holding bags full of coins, both silver and gold. In other boxes were jewels, ornaments, embroidered silks and velvets, and rare furs.

The southern square tower was the kitchen for cooking and roasting in winter-time only. The second chamber was the pantry, where all the venison pies, pastry, and bread were kept for emergency stores. The top floor was the buttery, or store-house, where were kept meal, flour, honey, spices, and other things used for cooking and eating. This last room was entered from the outside by winding stairs. Beneath the towers were the cellars for wines and ales. Except in winter this inner court was deserted most of the time, for in spring, summer, and autumn out-law life was out-of-doors.

Cooking was done in great clay ovens built over holes in the ground, where the wood-fires were lighted. General work and cleaning was done on long tables roofed over with thatched straw and reeds as a protection from rain. On rainy days the band ate under shelter, but in fair weather the food was best enjoyed served on the grassy turf.

When Robin was fully restored, after his bout with Arthur-a-Bland, and as vigorous as ever, he was in such a jolly mood that he made a vow to have a feast and invite some noble guest to share it. Early that morning some spies had brought news—the Bishop of Hereford with a numerous retinue would pass by the forest that day on his way to Nottingham town. Thereat Robin was full glad, for, since the fat Bishop had lost his

ROBIN HOOD

golden chain at Allan-a-Dale's wedding, he had threatened many a time to have Robin hanged, should he chance to catch him, to the nearest tree. And so it was that the Bishop, who traveled much, never went abroad without a troop of men-at-arms. Robin knew of the threat against him but cared not a whit. Only he took good care to find out what road the Bishop would follow in passing by the forest. On this bright, sunshiny morning he called together half a dozen stout companions and said to them:

"Come, kill me a good fat deer. I mean this day to have company to dine with me, and the Bishop of Hereford will be among them. I'll warrant he shall pay well for his cheer."

Then Robin and six of his men, all dressed as shepherds, started off in quest of a fat buck, which they shot and carried to the highway side. Straightway they skinned it, dressed it, and made a fire ready for cooking; but they let the carcass lie by the roadside, waiting till the Bishop should come riding by. At last the Bishop came along, decked out in all his fine attire (for he was a very vain man), with his men-at-arms in the rear. When he saw the shepherds, and what they had done, he called out in no friendly tone:

"What is the matter, ye thieving knaves, and for whom do ye make such a feast? Can it be that a few base hinds have the hardihood to kill the King's deer and carouse by the wayside? Who are ye, and how dare ye place your lives in such jeopardy?"

"We are poor shepherds, your lordship," quoth Robin, "who work hard at keeping sheep all the year round without any flesh food, and now have a mind to be merry for once by killing one of the King's fat deer."

"Ye are bold villains," roared the Bishop, "and I will make it my business to acquaint the King with these high doings. Therefore come with me forthwith, and pick up the deer, for before the King ye shall surely go."

"Oh, pardon!" said bold Robin Hood. "For it becomes not your lordship's coat to take so many lives away."

"Pardon, forsooth, ye wretched varlets!" quoth the Bishop. "No pardon do I owe thee. Wherefore should I pardon such

ROBIN HOOD

wanton mischief? The land has come to a pretty pass when even shepherds crave to live like barons!"

Just at that moment one of his retainers whispered to him, "That same base churl is Robin Hood in disguise."

Thereat the Bishop's red face turned white, and he trembled as if about to fall from his palfrey. None the less, he soon plucked up courage and boldly shouted to his men-at-arms to surround Robin and his comrades that they might catch him alive and bring him to the dungeon in Nottingham Castle. But Robin was too quick for them. Setting his back against a tree, he drew from beneath his shepherd's smock his silver bugle; and, putting it to his mouth, he blew a loud blast that reached far and wide. This loud call affrighted the men-at-arms, for they knew its meaning and feared that just as they were about to carry off Robin his outlaw band would attack them and slay them without mercy. So they stood stock still and heeded not the Bishop's orders.

"How now, my men-at-arms!" he cried, angrily. "Seize the villains at once!"

Just at that moment the soldiers saw threescore and ten of bold Robin's men come tripping o'er the lea, and without more ado they set their horses at a gallop and scampered off like rats before the housewife's broom, leaving the Bishop to wonder how he should get himself out of this sorry pickle. All the outlaws filed in a row before Robin and made obeisance to him, making as pretty a sight as the Bishop had e'er seen. Then Little John said:

"What is the matter, my brave master, that thou blowest so loud and hastily?"

"Oh, matter enow," cried Robin Hood. "Here is the Bishop of Hereford, and no pardon shall we have from him."

"Cut off his head, master," quoth Little John, "and throw him into his grave."

"Oh, pardon," said the Bishop. "For if I had known it had been you, I would have gone some other way."

"No pardon do I owe thee," quoth bold Robin Hood. "Did

ROBIN HOOD

I not, proud Bishop, ask pardon of thee but a little while agone, and didst thou not bid thy brave followers to take me and bring me to the King? Why should I now pardon thee? Therefore make haste and come with me, for to merry Sherwood thou shalt surely go as mine honored guest."

So the Bishop made the best of a bad matter, and they all set out for the trysting-place, the outlaws carrying the carcass of the deer on their shoulders. Robin took the Bishop's horse by the bridle and led him along the woodland path till they arrived at the great oak. Quoth the Bishop:

"I have much business in Nottingham this night that will not stay my waiting. Moreover, I am in no need of victuals or drink."

"No matter," said Robin. "Thou shalt sup with me to-night, whether thou likest or not, but I'll warrant thou art hungry and athirst."

Now the Bishop was really very tired, hungry, and thirsty, yet withal he would gladly have escaped, for he knew that something more than a merry feast was toward. After a little delay the feast was spread, the Bishop being placed between Robin and Little John. The hot, smoking venison was set before them, and the Bishop forgot himself and his troubles so much as to say, "By the mass, it hath a savory smell."

"Yea," laughed Little John, "and the wine will please thy palate as well."

When the Bishop had stuffed himself with meat and drink, he shouted out: "Come, my merry masters, bring the reckoning, that I may pay for this most excellent feast. Methinks, if it goes on much longer, the score will grow wondrous high."

"Lend me your purse, good Bishop," quoth Little John, "and I'll tell you the price of the feast by and by." Then Little John took the Bishop's cloak and spread it upon the greensward, and, turning the purse upside down, poured forth a clinking stream of golden coins.

"Here's money enough, master," quoth he, "to pay the reckoning, and 'tis a comely sight to see. Let us count the coins; such a full purse makes me feel charitable toward the Bishop, though I warrant he loveth me not so heartily." When the money was counted they found it to be just three hundred pounds.

"Pick it up carefully," said Robin, "and go place it in my treasury. To the Bishop we will return the empty purse. In sooth, when he getteth more money he will have a pouch to keep it, ready for our next merry meeting."

Then they took the Bishop by the hand, and bade Allan-a-Dale to play lively music upon his harp. Hand in hand, they made the fat old Bishop dance in his boots round and round the oak-tree. At last, both tired and weary, he was set upon his horse. Robin told off two men for guides; and the Bishop, glad indeed to get away, was soon jogging through the forest on his way to Nottingham town.

Later the outlaws learned from a spy that the Bishop's urgent business in Nottingham was to receive church tithes and doles gathered from certain lands and property held by him round-about Nottingham town. Angry and ill-tempered toward every one of his men, whom he found awaiting him, he conceived it his first duty to keep dinning loud complaints into the ears of the poor, half-distracted Sheriff. After patiently listening to the tale the Sheriff made answer:

"I tell thee, pious Bishop, if thou lovest thy skin and dost wish to keep it whole, the next time thou goest upon the highway nigh Sherwood, turn neither to the right nor the left. Bid thy men march straight on, and tarry not."

"But," interrupted the Bishop, "if we see a pack of rascals feeding and feasting on the King's deer by the wayside, we must in the King's name protect his own."

"Nay, nay, by our Good Lady, thou art wrong. This sly fox knows our doings, our goings and comings. He doth devise all manner of disguises, wicked plots, and audacious schemes to encompass thee and thy money. No matter if thou shouldst espy the King bound to a tree, thy best course would be e'en to let the King care for his own; for I'll warrant it to be a stuffed

"HERE'S MONEY ENOUGH MASTER," QUOTH LITTLE
JOHN, "TO PAY THE RECKONING"

ROBIN HOOD

image of his majesty. When thou dost journey through the country hereabout, go with empty purse and in plain attire. Let thy servants carry thy gold."

"Nay, by the mass!" quoth the Bishop. "They are greater thieves than Robin Hood."

"Hast thou, good Bishop, no trusty followers to carry thy wealth?"

"None so trusty as myself," said the Bishop.

"Then in good sooth," said the Sheriff, "I am at a loss to advise thee, unless thou likest to return home by another road, which perchance may baffle the villain and his band."

That night the Bishop rested with Friar Bertrand—a sly, unsavory man, with wide jaws and wicked little black eyes, who lived by his wits. This Bertrand was by far too timid to attempt aught against the Bishop, but he was glib of tongue and ready with advice.

"If your Grace goes the other way, that will be just what the outlaw will expect you to do. Therefore go back the same way as you came. Such a bold act will deceive the villain."

"Thou saist truly," quoth the Bishop; and the next morning, sure enough, he started back on the road by which he had come. Now it chanced that this Bertrand had a servant just as false as his master, who acted as a spy; and he gave the outlaws warning of the Bishop's new plans. The next morning was bright and sun-shiny, and Robin was taking a stroll through the forest by himself. He had bidden a number of his comrades to go by another path and meet him on the highway. Presently he was aware of strangers approaching, but could not see them through the thick maze of woodland trees. Then he bethought him, "If I stay any longer, alone as I am, I shall be taken prisoner." So off he ran down a path.

The strangers proved to be the Bishop and his company of soldiers, who at once recognized Robin by his green mantle. Seeing that he was alone, they gave chase and pressed closely behind him. Robin turned about and chanced to spy a little cottage, into which he ran crying out to the old wife:

ROBIN HOOD

"Haste thee, good dame, and give me means to save my life."

"Why, who art thou?" said the old woman. "Come, tell me, for thine own good."

"I am an outlaw; many do call me by the name of Robin Hood. Out yonder is the Bishop of Hereford, with his men-at-arms, who would fain take me. If they do, the Bishop hath sworn to hang me on the limb of a tree."

"If thou art Robin Hood," said the good old wife, "as I am full sure thou art, I will make some means to foil the Bishop and all his company. For I remember one Saturday night thou didst bring me both shoon and hosen. Therefore, I will hide thee and keep thee from thine enemies."

"Then give me thy old coat of gray," said Robin, "and take thou my mantle of green, and I will take up thy spindle and twine in exchange for my bow and arrow." Thus arrayed, bold Robin issued forth, passing by the Bishop's soldiers, to join his comrades by the wayside; and as he drew nigh them Little John spied him coming along the glade.

"See, my merry men," cried he, "that old witch stalking along the path. I will let fly an arrow that she may do no more harm to little children."

"Hold thy hand," shouted Robin. "I am thy good master, Robin Hood, arrayed thus to escape the Bishop's men."

Meanwhile the Bishop in a furious voice called out to the old woman: "We saw that traitor thief, Robin Hood, enter thy cottage. Let us search, or bring him unto us."

The frightened old woman then opened the cottage door; and the Bishop, upon seeing a figure dressed in a mantle of green, holding a bow, dragged her out and placed her on a milk-white steed and rode beside her on a dapple-gray mare. Chuckling and laughing with great glee at so easy a capture of the bold outlaw, the Bishop said:

"By my faith, this will be joyful news for the Sheriff. We will ride back to Nottingham and place this precious rogue in a dungeon where he hath belonged this many a year—and nobody brave enough but a churchman to catch him!"

ROBIN HOOD

Thus talking and laughing, they rode along, till at length the Bishop spied a hundred brave bowmen standing in a line fronting on their path. Then quoth he:

"Oh, who are those men yonder that range within the woodland shade?"

"Marry," said the old woman, "I think it be Robin Hood and his merry men."

"God-a-mercy then," the Bishop cried, "who art thou which I have here by my side?"

"Why, I am an old woman; look on my long gray hair," cried she.

"Woe is me," said the Bishop, "that ever I saw this day!"

When the Bishop's company saw the bold array of the outlaw band come marching forth, with Little John at their head, they straightway scurried off to hide, as they had done before, leaving the Bishop once more alone. Even the old woman rode off on the Bishop's white steed without being noticed, so frightened he was at this sudden turn of fortune.

"Take courage, good Bishop," said Robin, "and get off thy horse while I tie it to a tree; for I see thy purse is wondrous fat, and would fain know what is in it." Then he took off his mantle and spread it on the ground.

"Now," quoth Little John, laughing, "let us see the purse."

So they turned it over and found five hundred pounds of good money.

"Now he can go," said Robin.

"Nay," quoth Little John, "that may not be, for I vow before he leaves us he shall sing a mass to us and our good outlaw band."

The Bishop obeyed their order in a most doleful tone of voice. Then they set him upon his horse backward and gave him the tail for a bridle, sending six stout fellows to guide him to the road, where he could again meet his men and go upon his way.

XV

ROBIN HOOD AND THE BEGGAR

ROBIN HOOD had been outlawed when he was only fifteen years old—in other words, officers and soldiers of the Crown could kill him at sight without a trial. Of his own free will he chose to lead such a life in defiance of the law. At the age of thirty-five he had gathered about him a large band of brave followers who would, one and all, shed their last drop of blood for him if need were. Wise and just he was in his dealings, oft-times charitable to the poor and needy, brave and dangerous in fight. The rich barons and churchmen who ground the faces of the poor trembled at his very name. What he took from those that fell in his way he did not waste, but found good means—as you will see later—to help many who were sadly in need of succor. His love of adventure did not wane with the passing years; and, though he needed no more men for his band, he was just as ready as ever to test the bravery in fair fight of all who crossed his path.

Now it fell upon a fair afternoon that Robin went alone through a fern-clad forest path. After a while he got upon the highroad, where he met a beggar going sturdily along at a good pace, looking neither to the right nor to the left, noticing no one as he strode on his way. In his hand he held a pike-staff that was both stout and strong, while wound about his body was a clouted cloth folded many times, making an excellent covering from wind and rain. Tied to a leathern strap there hung from his neck a large meal-bag, firmly fastened to a stout, broad buckle, and upon his head were three hats stuck fast together, one above the other, so that wherever he went little did he care either for sun or for rain.

When good Robin spied this oddly attired stranger he stepped boldly right in front of him, for he had a shrewd thought that the beggar was not so poor as he seemed.

"Tarry," quoth Robin. "Tarry awhile and speak with me."

But the beggar, making as if he had not heard him, went but the faster on his way, without so much as a turn of his head.

"Marry," said Robin, "thou showest me scant courtesy. Thou must tarry, for I have somewhat to say to thee."

"By my three hats," cried the beggar, in a harsh voice, "to tarry I have no will, for it groweth late, and it is yet far to my lodging-house. Should they have supper before I get there, perchance my stomach shall go bare of food."

"Now, by my troth," said good Robin, "I see well that in thinking only of thine own supper, thou hast no care of mine. All this day have I eaten no food, and wot not where to lie this night. To the tavern would I go, but in sooth I have no money. Sir stranger, you must lend me some till we meet again."

The beggar answered peevishly: "I have no money to lend; methinks thou art as young as I and as strong, I warrant. If thou dost fast till I lend thee money, thou shalt eat naught this year."

"Then," said bold Robin, "by my troth, since we are together here, if thou hast but a clipt farthing I'll take it from thee ere thou go. Come, beggar, lay down thy clouted cloth and cease to stand there staring me in the face; for I will open up all thy bags, thy tag-rags and bobtails, and rip them to

ROBIN HOOD

pieces with my hands. Shouldst thou make an outcry, I vow by the saints to try how far a broad arrow can pierce a beggar's skin."

The beggar looked at Robin with a wry smile upon his face and made answer thus:

"Far better let me be; for do not think I care a straw, or be afeard for thy nip-crooked tree that thou call'st a bow, nor that I care any whit for thy curn sticks that thou call'st arrows, which are no more, in sooth, than skewers to fasten up a pudding bag withal. Here do I defy thee to do me harm—for all thy loud talk thou wilt get nothing from me but ill."

Such fearless words from a ragged beggar roused Robin's wrath. Straightway he nocked a broad arrow and bent his great bow. But e'er 'twas drawn a span, the beggar with his stout pike-staff reached forward with so swift a stroke that the bow burst in twain. Nothing daunted, Robin with a bound darted to strike down the beggar with his sword, but that proved likewise vain, for the fellow with his pike-staff struck such a fierce blow on Robin's hand that his sword fell to the ground.

Good Robin could not speak a word, for he was sick at heart and faint from bitter pain. Unable either to fight or to flee, he knew not what to do. Yet still the beggar with his terrible pike-staff laid lusty blows upon his side and back, till at last Robin fell down on the soft sward in a swoon, lying helpless and bleeding at the mercy of his terrible foe.

"Stand up, stand up," the beggar man said; " 'tis a shame to go to rest. In truth, I think it were best to stay till thou gettest thy money. Then go to the tavern and buy both food and wine with the beggar's money. There thou canst boast of what thou didst get in the forest."

Good Robin answered ne'er a word, but lay still as a stone. Closed were both his eyes, and his cheeks were pale as any clay. With a few more blows upon his body the beggar thought him dead, and leaving him to lie stark and still, his face upturned to the sky, he strode on his way.

Now it so happened that by good chance three of Robin's

Ye cruel BEGGAR

ROBIN HOOD

band came walking by the way and found their master lying on the ground, wounded, bleeding, and senseless.

"Who hath done this foul deed, comrades?" said one. "Let us take our dear master up, and carry him to yon brook, that we may sprinkle water on his face and so bring him to life." So they took up good Robin, who made a piteous moan, while blood gushed forth from his mouth and nose. Yet though they searched all over his body, they found no cuts, but many cruel bruises. When his brow had been bathed with cold water, Robin at last came to his senses enough to speak a little.

"Tell us, dear master," said his men, "tell us what is the matter, and how thou didst fall into such an evil case."

Good Robin sighed deep e'er he began to tell of his disgrace. "For twenty years and more have I been outlaw and forester in this wood, yet I was never so hard bestead as ye have found me here. A beggar with a clouted cloak hath with his pike-staff so mauled my back that I fear 'twill never be well. He went o'er yon hill, and upon his head he carried three hats. If e'er ye loved your master, go now to revenge me of this vile deed and bring him back to me again. Take care that he escape you not, for if ye cannot bring him to me, 'twere a great shame upon us all."

"One of us shall stay with thee because thou art in no state to be left alone, and the other two, I warrant, shall bring the villain beggar back to use as thou listest."

"Now, by my faith," said good Robin, "enough has been said. Take good heed, for I fear me ye will both be evil a-paid if he get a chance to swing his wicked tree around your noddles."

"Be not afraid, dear master, that we two can be bested by any base beggar that carries naught but a staff! Thou shalt shortly see that his staff will stand him in no stead. He shall be brought back again, fast bound, to see if thou wilt have us slay him."

"Be sly, then," said Robin, "and by stealth work your way into his path before he is aware. Then pounce upon him, and first of all lay hands on his staff."

ROBIN HOOD

The two outlaws then left Robin, clinging to a tree, like a poor, tottering old man. Now the beggar had mended his pace and was striding along over the hill, giving no thought to the trouble he had caused and only anxious to reach his lodging ere nightfall. The two outlaws ran at full speed by a lower path, careless of the mud and briars along the way, going a distance of over three miles. Then, turning to a little clump of bushes in a glen that the beggar must surely pass, they hid themselves close behind trees on each side of the path, standing ready till the beggar drew nigh. After a little they saw him coming, and just as he got betwixt them both leaped upon him. One gripped the pike-staff; and the other, with drawn dagger at his breast, cried:

"False and bloody knave, quit thy staff, or thou shalt need a priest. Stir but a hair under thy three hats and, by Saint Wilfrid, I will drive this dirk to the hilt in thy black heart."

Taken off his guard, the beggar was so affrighted that he dared not move. He could not run, he could not wield his staff. He was not sure but other outlaws might be near; so in despair, thinking that at last his life's end was near at hand, he began to crave mercy.

"Grant me my life," he pleaded, "and hold away that ugly knife. I never harmed you in all my life, neither by night nor day, and indeed you do a great sin if you slay a poor silly beggar."

"Thou liest, false and cruel varlet," cried the outlaw who held his staff. "Thou hast near slain the gentlest and kindest man that e'er was born. Back again to him thou shalt be led, fast bound with thongs, to see if he will have thee slain or bid us hang thee on a tree."

Then the beggar thought that all was done with him, though if he could but escape out of their hands and get hold of his staff he was sure that he would teach them another game. While they made ready to bind him he cudgeled his brains for some wily scheme to free himself. The only way that came into his mind was to tempt them with money; so he said:

THE BEGGAR FLUNG THE MEAL IN THEIR FACES

ROBIN HOOD

"Brave gentlemen, be good to me, and let me go. It helps you not a flea to take a beggar's blood. 'Twas but to save mine own hide that I did hurt your master, and listen, good friends—I will give you a recompense that shall make you rich if you will but set me free and do me no more harm. I will give you a hundred pounds, and much more odd silver that I have gathered these many years. Under this clouted cloak I have it, far hidden beneath its folds next to my skin and eke in the bottom of my meal-bag."

To this neither of the young men answered a word, but each looked at his companion to see whether he would be false to his honor and disgrace the band. One argued, "We will take the money to our captain and tell him that the beggar is slain." The other said, "Our orders were 'Bring him back alive or dead.'" At last they agreed to yield to the beggar's counsel and let him go, then follow after and take him again by stealth when they had his money; for, being swift of foot, they might easily overtake him.

"False knave," said one, "say no more, but get the money and count it out. 'Tis little enough to pay for the ill turn thou hast done our master; yet come what may, if thou dost give us the money now we will not take thee back."

So the beggar thanked them right heartily, and straightway set about loosening his clouted cloak to spread it on the ground. Then he took from his neck a bag containing over two pecks of meal, which he set down upon the cloak. Opening wide the bag, he bent down and felt in every nook and corner for the money. Both young men drew their faces closer to see the gold appear, when of a sudden the beggar lifted out two great handfuls of meal and flung it in their faces, blinding them so that they could do naught with their hands save strive to wipe the meal from eyes, nose, and mouth. In a trice the beggar grasped his pike-staff and, with a gleeful laugh, cried:

"Now, my pretty pair of blades, if I've done you wrong in mealing of your clothes, with my staff I will strike off the meal again."

With that, he began to ply his staff, filling the air with meal from their bodies as his mighty blows fell on their shoulders, necks, and arms. The young outlaws, half blinded and choked, could do naught to help themselves. They turned and ran with all the speed they could muster, leaving the beggar shaking his staff in the air and calling upon them to stay awhile and get well dusted.

"What's all this haste?" he cried. "May not you tarry still? I'll pay you with a right good will until ye have had enough and to spare. The shakings of my meal-bag have by chance blown into your eyes, but what of that? I have a good pike-staff that will soon make them clear."

Thus he went on entreating them in right loving fashion to tarry, but the young outlaws heard him not, for they were far away. Since the night was creeping on apace, it would be vain to follow and attack him now, so they thought it wise to return, and with sad hearts and downcast looks they got them back to their master.

"Well, my comrades," asked Robin, "how did ye speed in your quest?"

They answered him, "Full ill, and we were evil a-paid."

"That cannot be," quoth Robin. "A man would think to look at your clothes that ye have been working for the miller. Tell me the matter truly—how ye fared, and what ye have done with the bold beggar I sent you for but now."

The young men drooped down, hanging their heads for very shame, and could not speak a word. Then, with true anger in his voice, Robin said:

"Because I fell beneath the cudgel of this beggar fiend I think ye feared he would serve you in the same fashion."

At these words, so true and so just, the young men confessed, and told Robin the truth all to the end — how the beggar blinded them with the meal, how he basted their bones so sore to dust it from their clothes, and how they fled to the forest.

Good Robin cried out: "Fie, fie for shame! We are dis-

ROBIN HOOD

honored forevermore. Help me to lift my weary bones, and take me quickly to my bower."

As they carried him along the path he thought he would full fain have revenge, yet even in his pain he smiled to think that two of his merry young men had gotten a taste of that beggar's pike-staff besides himself.

XVI

ROBIN SELLS POTS AND DISHES

ROBIN was angered to the depths of his heart at thought of the beggar's brutishness, for he himself had never in his life struck a fallen foe, to say nothing of beating a man who lay senseless and helpless at his feet. Yet anon he bethought him: "In sooth, I was to blame! I brought it upon mine own head, and must perforce bear the pain I got." Such were his thoughts as he painfully dragged his aching bones along, with the help of his two followers, back through the forest to the oak glade. It seemed an age before he got there, and twice he fainted from weakness. Little John met them with a very sad face, and he wept to see his master in such a plight. Then with his strong arms he fairly carried Robin to his bower, there to lie a month or more till his swollen, bruised body grew strong and well once more.

Many a time he bemoaned himself bitterly to Little John because he could not go abroad. Then, with comforting words, mixed with a spice of sound advice, Little John would soothe him, saying:

"In truth, my dear master, thou art too prone to fight with

ROBIN HOOD COMPETES AT FINSBURY FIELD

Page 256

THE AILING ROBIN HOOD WITH THE ABBESS OF KIRKLEY
Page 282

quarter-staff against a foe more used to that weapon. With thy good long-bow, the case is different, for thou would'st ever be the victor."

"I cannot in cold blood," quoth Robin, "send a shaft through a foe's body with but a pace or two between us. Once I slew a man, and ne'er again will I take life save at dire need or in the heat of combat. But, by the mass, I will no longer lie here like a cat tied in a bag."

Again Little John would gently chide his master, bidding him wait at least till he could stand upon his legs without wabbling. "For," said he, "our treasure is ample, our wants are all supplied, and the men content. Be patient, therefore, for in a week or more, once again thou wilt be strong—long before the wintry wind blows through the glade."

At last, toward the end of summer, the three best leeches of the band—Friar Tuck, Arthur-a-Bland, and Little John—agreed that Robin was well enough to go upon short trips to hunt the deer. Shooting contests were held and games resumed, as a change from the more serious work of gathering in the winter stores. It was now the middle of August. The days were warm, the evenings long and light till ten o'clock, so that the band was in a merry mood, as was their wont when all went well.

Thus it was that, on the next day, a bright, fair morn, being a Saturday and a market-day, Robin, Little John, and others of the band set forth toward the great highway that ran along the forest edge, to gather tolls from any that were able to pay, and give away, for charity's sake, to those in dire need. Anon they saw a man sitting on the shafts of a rude little cart pulled by a pony. The cart was filled with mugs, basins, and other pottery vessels, which the man bought very cheap at Stoke, where they were made, and carted from town to town to sell at a good profit. He was singing a merry ditty, now and then whipping up his pony that he might reach Nottingham market in good time. It was plain by his looks that he could take good care of his pots as well as himself.

ROBIN HOOD

"Yonder comes a stout potter," quoth jolly Robin, "that hath crossed this forest many a time, yet hath never paid one penny of passage money to us. He shall not escape us this time, I warrant."

"Better let him pass, good master," said Little John. "I met the fellow once at Wentbridge, and he gave me three such clouts that I want no more from him, though I gave him clout for clout. I will lay forty shillings there is not a man among us that can make the potter pay toll."

Bold Robin could not let that pass. "Here are forty shillings," he cried, "and more will I lay that I can make that bold potter pay some token for his passage."

"He will give thee his staff for a token! I vow that from him thou wilt get no other pay, my master," said John. But Robin, without more words, strode to the middle of the highroad, and, standing firm as a rock till the potter drew nigh, laid his hand on the bridle, bidding the man stand.

"Fellow," bawled the potter, "what is thy will?"

"All these three years and more, potter," quoth Robin, "thou hast passed by this way, yet never hast been so courteous as to pay a penny of toll to us."

"What is thy name?" said the potter, "and what is thy right to ask for passage money of me on the King's highway?"

"Robin Hood is my name, and king of these woods am I, to whom it is thy bounden duty to pay toll."

"Not a bad farthing shalt thou get from me," said the potter. "Let go thy hand from my horse, or I vow to strike it off with my staff." Straightway leaping down from the shaft, he unstrapped from under the cart a stout pike-staff, saying in angry tones: "Now, bold outlaw, take thy hand from my horse."

Robin drew his sword and, with a buckler upon his arm, advanced to meet the potter, who with a powerful balk-stroke smote off the shield. In a trice the naughty pike-staff was brought down with another fierce blow on Robin's neck as he stooped to get his buckler again. So stiff was the stroke that it sent Robin sprawling on the ground.

ROBIN HOOD

"Let us go to help our master," cried Little John, "or yon potter will do him harm."

Then, running toward Robin, with shouts of laughter, he said: "Who has won the wager now? Shall I have the forty shillings, or shall ye, master, have mine?"

"Yea, were they a hundred shillings," said Robin, "in faith, they are all thine."

"There is little courtesy," said the potter, "as I have heard wise men say, to take from a poor yeoman what little he hath while driving along the highway."

"By my faith, thou saist true," said Robin, "and from this day forth thou shalt never be hindered; for a friendship would I have with thee, and good payment will I give. Make exchange with me of thy clothing, for I will sell pots in Nottingham town, and thou shalt stay here in the forest to feast on good venison. When I come back, if I sell all, thine shall be the gain."

"Marry, to that I will agree," quoth the potter. "Thou shalt find me an honest fellow; and if thou canst sell my pots well, come back again when thou dost list."

Then spake Little John and his comrades, saying: "Master, take care and beware of the Sheriff, for he would gladly slay thee by fair means or foul. Alone, thou shalt be in great jeopardy."

"Nay, my good comrades," quoth Robin, "let me be, for by the help of our Good Lady to Nottingham will I go."

So Robin changed clothes with the potter, and, with some touches here and there to make a better disguise, he jumped on the shaft of the cart and drove away in a jolly mood, singing a merry song. When he reached Nottingham, he drew up his horse close by the Sheriff's gate, and gave it some oats and hay. Then setting forth his pots, both large and small, upon the cart, so as to make the best show, he began to cry out:

"Crocks and pots, jugs and mugs, who wants to buy? I give one extra, no matter how large or small."

This way of bargaining was new to the wives and widows of Nottingham, and soon drew a large crowd round his cart. Not content with throwing in an extra pot, Robin sold pots worth

ROBIN HOOD

five pence for three pence. This made the women gape, both old and young; and while they bought they said to each other, slyly, "This potter will never thrive at this rate."

"Thou wilt have none left ere long, if thou dost sell so cheap," said one buxom wife.

"For that cause came I hither," quoth smiling Robin, "to sell all I have." And he did sell so fast that before noon only five pieces were left.

"Well done, thou cunning potter," said Robin to himself. "These five unsold pots will I give with my compliments to the Sheriff's wife." And so, in sooth, he did.

"Grammercy, sir," said the Sheriff's wife, with a tender smile on good Robin. "When thou dost come to this town again I shall buy what pots I want from you, so much do I like thy courtesy. Thy kindness is truly great, and I would that thou mightest come and dine with the Sheriff and me."

"God's mercy, good lady," said Robin, "thy bidding shall be done."

Then a young maid carried in the pots, and Robin followed the Sheriff's wife to the hall, where he met the Sheriff, who spake him fair.

"Look," quoth the lady, "what this potter hath given thee and me for a present—five pots, both large and small."

"He is full welcome," said the Sheriff. "Let us enter and go to dine."

As they sat at the table, with merry talk and laughter, two of the Sheriff's men began to speak of a prize of forty shillings offered for the best shooting with the long-bow among the towns-people that day. "Now, as I am a true Christian man," Robin said to himself, "this shooting-match will I see."

When they had appeased their hunger upon the very best of bread, ale, and wine, to the shooting-butts they all went to see who would win the prize. The Sheriff's men began to shoot, but they were very poor archers, and none of them got nearer the mark than half the length of a long-bow. The potter looked on with great contempt; and when the Sheriff said, "What

"I GIVE ONE EXTRA, NO MATTER HOW LARGE OR SMALL"

ROBIN HOOD

thinkest thou, good potter, of our archery?" he made answer: "In plain truth, it seemeth to me to be very vile. An I had a bow, with one shot I would beat them all."

"I warrant thou shalt have a bow for that one shot," quoth the Sheriff, "the best thou mayst choose from such as we have. Thou seemest strong and stalwart as any here." He then bade a yeoman that stood by bring some bows for the potter to choose from.

"'Tis the best here," quoth Robin, as he took up a bow, "though in sooth 'tis a poor, weak thing. Nevertheless, with it I will make good my word."

So without more ado he strode up to the line, side by side with the Sheriff's men, who smiled and twitted him upon his impudence in daring to shoot in such company. The potter answered naught, but, pulling the string to his ear, he carelessly shot the arrow within a foot of the mark. Then the Sheriff's men tried once more with little better success. When the potter again took his place to shoot, they had greater respect for his skill and waited anxiously to see what he would do. Taking much more careful aim, he let fly the shaft and cleft the wand apart, much to the wonder of the Sheriff's men, who thought it great shame that a common potter should win the prize from them. But the Sheriff and his wife were both mightily pleased, and said to the potter:

"Thou art a man worthy to bear a bow in whatever place thou goest."

"In my cart," he made answer, "I have a bow that I had from Robin Hood."

"Knowest thou Robin Hood?" asked the surprised Sheriff. "Prithee, tell me of him."

"A hundred times," replied the potter, "have I shot with him under his trysting-tree."

"By my faith," quoth the Sheriff, "I would give a hundred pounds to have that villainous outlaw now stand before me here."

"I would fain win that hundred pounds," said the potter, "and to-morrow after we have taken our breakfast, if thou wilt boldly go with me, I will e'en show thee Robin Hood."

[181]

ROBIN HOOD

"I will requite thee well," said the Sheriff, joyfully. "By my faith, thou shalt not repent of serving me in this matter."

Upon the morrow the potter was early ready with horse and cart. Taking leave of the Sheriff's wife, he thanked her heartily for her good cheer.

"Good dame," quoth he, "for my love to you, be pleased to wear this gold ring."

"Grammercy, good sir, I yield to thy wish, for I trow the Sheriff's heart was never so light to see the fair forest as in the company of so gallant a companion."

So the Sheriff, on his horse, and the potter, seated in his little cart, both set off for Sherwood.

The morning was bright and warm, and the little birds sang merrily among the green leaves. "The greenwood is a merry place," said Robin, "for a man that has aught to spend, and by the sound of my horn we shall soon know if Robin Hood be near at hand." Then he set his horn to his mouth and blew a blast both loud and long, that could be heard far adown the forest glade.

"I hear my master's call," said Little John. "Let us haste, and run to see if all be well." Anon through an opening of the trees they appeared before the potter and addressed him, saying:

"Master, how hast thou fared in Nottingham? Hast thou sold all thy wares?"

"Yea, by my troth, Little John. Look thou and see. I have brought the Sheriff of Nottingham in exchange for my goods."

"He is full welcome," said Little John. "Such tidings make us glad."

'Twas then that the Sheriff saw the trick that the potter had served him, and he thought he would rather have given a hundred pounds than to have met Robin Hood that day.

"Had I known," quoth he, "that thou wert Robin Hood, thou shouldst not have seen this fair forest for a thousand years."

"That wot I well," said jolly Robin, laughing. "Therefore thou shalt leave thy horse and other gear with us. Hither thou camest a-horseback, and back thou shalt go afoot to give my greetings to thy good wife at home. I shall give her a white

ROBIN HOOD

palfrey, and thou mayst tell her that had she used less courtesy thou wouldst have fared much more sadly at our hands." Thus the Sheriff parted from Robin, and to Nottingham he took his way.

His wife was there to give him a welcome. "How didst thou fare in the greenwood?" she said. "And hast thou brought Robin home?"

The Sheriff swore a great oath and said: "I have been basely scorned, and tricked of all the moneys I took to the greenwood. My large, fine horse, its gold trappings, my pouch with a hundred pounds, were all stript from me amid the jeers and merry quips of that vile band."

Upon that, the good dame laughed loud and long. "Now," quoth she, "he has then been well paid for all those pots he gave to us."

So we leave the unhappy Sheriff and return to the greenwood, where Robin called the potter to him, saying, "Good potter, what were thy pots worth that I sold in Nottingham market?"

Quoth the potter: "They were worth two pounds, but I should have traded and made more by my traffic."

"Thou shalt have ten pounds," said jolly Robin. "And remember, bold potter, when thou comest to the greenwood thou shalt ever be welcome."

So they parted as the best of friends, each well satisfied with the other. Then the potter set off blithe and merry on his way back to Stoke to get his cart refilled with pots and crocks, hoping to make as good a trade again. "But of that," quoth he, "I have grave doubts—there is but one Robin Hood."

XVII

ROBIN AND SIR GUY OF GISBOURNE

THIS latest clever trick of Robin Hood's was the last straw that broke the Sheriff's patience. He wept and sobbed; he wailed and sighed full sore. Each man that sat at meat with him or passed him upon the streets of Nottingham town seemed to be Robin Hood in disguise. The disgrace was so much the harder to bear because his wife found delight in constantly talking of the comely, courteous outlaw and his present of the gold ring, which she still wore. So the Sheriff longed for a dire revenge, and searched eagerly for some means whereby he might put an end at once and forever to the troubles he had borne for twenty-odd years.

At last he bethought him to give a great feast and invite as many as would come of the barons and knights of the shire. For he thought that if they would not help him with money and men they might at least advise him how best to rid the near-by forests of these pests. He had oft tried to get the aid of bold yeomen of his town, but they had flatly said him nay, for many of them had received kindness from Robin and his men. So the Sheriff bade his servants prepare a great feast, to which came not a few of the barons and knights.

ROBIN HOOD

When they had eaten of the good things and drunk well of the wine, the Sheriff arose and addressed them, laying bare all his woe. Thereat one brave knight got upon his feet and said:

"Sir Sheriff, while we grieve with thee in this trouble, not one of us can soil his knightly hands to draw sword in so mean a cause—to wit, the catching of a rascally deer-stealer. Such base deeds are meet for thy yeomen or the King's foresters."

"Oft have I promised them much gold," quoth the Sheriff, "but they either will not or dare not encounter this band. Yea, they all turn pale at the name of Robin Hood."

"In faith," quoth the knight, "I know not any other means whereby thou canst have thy will unless, haply, some knight down at the heels for want of friends and gold were willing to lead a company of trained men to the forest and drive the out-laws away."

"Dost thou, Sir Knight, know of such a one?"

"There is one," replied the knight, "who would do thy bid-ding, if the prize were great. This Sir Guy of Gisbourne is bold enough to do any deed thou mayst set for him, nor will he value his knightly honor above five hundred pounds."

After the guests had gone the Sheriff lost no time in seeking out this Sir Guy, and on the morrow he sent a messenger on horse-back to the little market-town of Gisbourne in the west Riding of Yorkshire. Now Sir Guy was poor; he had wasted his sub-stance in riotous living; but, instead of repenting, he was ever ready to do any deed, however base, not only because he needed gold, but for the mere love of doing evil.

In his native town he was feared by every man, and ab-horred by every wife, widow, or lass. Besides his wickedness he was the ugliest creature in merry England. His naturally savage features were scarred by many wounds and cuts, for he had been to the wars in the Holy Land, in Ireland, in Scotland, and in the South. Everywhere he went, ever fighting; yet he seemed to bear a charmed life. Utterly cruel, with a black and stony heart, his bold and fierce demeanor affrighted all men. When he was angry, his face and scars turned a livid blue, so awful to

ROBIN HOOD

look upon that his foes took him for a demon risen from the regions below. It was his wont to go clad from head to foot in the hide of a horse. The ears stood up from a hood, back of which hung the mane, and below was the horse's tail. This body-covering was tanned soft with the hair outside, so that he who wore it looked more a beast than a man. Such, then, was the evil Sir Guy, whom the Sheriff's messenger went to seek as a leader to fight and destroy the good and kind Robin Hood and his merry outlaws.

When he reached the little town of Gisbourne, the messenger had little trouble in learning the whereabouts of him he sought.

"What is the price?" roared Sir Guy, when he had heard the tale. "Repeat to me the sum, that I be not mistaken."

"Five hundred pounds in good coin," said the messenger, "for the living body of Robin Hood, or his head if thou slayest him."

" 'Tis a fair sum for so slight a deed," said Sir Guy, slowly, "and, to be brief, I will do the Sheriff's will. The outlaw's head is mine; the money is earned. Dost thou hear that?" Down came his fist with such a crack on the table that the messenger nearly jumped out of his skin.

"Yea, Sir Guy, I hear, and doubt it not."

"Well for thee thou hast no doubts. What, ho! knavish hind!" he shouted to a servant. "Get my horse, and furnish him for combat. Get me my two Irish daggers and my longest brown Egyptian blade. There is work afoot for us, so choose the toughest yew long-bow and double-pointed shafts, and be ready anon."

All was soon in readiness, and ere long the two were riding back toward Nottingham, which they reached late on the following day. Meanwhile, the Sheriff had not been idle. He foresaw that Sir Guy would willingly do a work so much to his taste, especially for a prize so large. He had already gathered together a hundred of his own men and two hundred of the King's foresters. The latter he would place under the command of Sir Guy, and he himself would lead his own servants. He was no coward, to say sooth, though his men were not of the same metal.

ROBIN HOOD

When the knight presented himself, the Sheriff's joy was unbounded. "Such a fierce-looking monster did I ne'er behold," he thought. "Surely he will slay bold Robin." Then he said aloud: "Thrice welcome art thou, Sir Knight of Gisbourne. Let us dine and then talk of what we have to do."

So they went into the hall, where Sir Guy seated himself opposite the place where the Sheriff's wife would sit. Unsheathing his two Irish daggers, he laid one shining blade close beside his platter, the other beside his wine-goblet, and prepared to eat. The Sheriff's wife had been told of this man, and what he was about to do, but she was so affrighted at the knives and the fellow's evil looks that she fainted dead away in the arms of her husband, who helped the servants to carry her away from the table.

"What is the matter with thy good lady, Sir Sheriff?" asked Guy.

"In sooth," said he, "she is overcome with joy to know that the outlaw's end is near."

"Ay, by the bones of Saint Withold!" growled Sir Guy, "of a truth it is so. But tell me, what manner of man is this Robin Hood, famed as he is so far and wide? Is he big of bone and broad of chest, like King Richard, that all men fear him?"

"Nay, by the mass," quoth the Sheriff, "he is as mild as a sucking pig and gentle as a lamb. Marry, the cooing turtle-dove could not match him in soft persuasion. But mark thee well, Sir Knight, no fox was ever so sly; no adder creeping through the damp sward is so silent as his footfall on the grass."

"And what of his prowess?" asked Sir Guy. "I have heard of his skill in archery, but doubt it."

"Doubt it not, Sir Knight, for no archer liveth, nor ever lived, that can match him. With the broadsword and buckler, and eke with the quarter-staff, he hath met in combat the strongest and best in merry England, and he hath drawn them to his band. I know not of any means to take him save to outnumber him. Outwit him—'tis impossible! Outfight him—'tis doubtful! Haply if thou canst meet him alone, thou mayst have the

ROBIN HOOD

better of him. Indeed, rather would I see it done in such a manner than in any other. Therefore it were well that thou shouldst go before us to tempt the wily fox, if that may be, to single combat. It is well known that he loves such fights; and many, so I hear, have met him, hand to hand, alone in divers parts of the forest."

"Truly," said the Knight, "the thieving rogue hath affrighted all the bravery out of Nottinghamshire. Nevertheless, I will do as thou biddest. A blast from this horn shall tell that he is dead. But come, good Sheriff, we tarry over-long. Rest assured that Robin Hood shall meet his end before the moon doth cast her beams through the forest leaves."

So the Sheriff gave command, and soon his three hundred stalwart yeomen and foresters stood ready to follow the two leaders, who, both on horseback, rode in front on their way through the forest to destroy the outlaws' nest.

On that very same morning, just before sunrise, you might have seen all of Robin's merry men wrapped snugly in their night-cloaks, fast asleep on the grassy sward, round about the great oak. On a low-hanging branch above Robin's head sat a throstle, singing so loud that it roused him from his sleep. Half raising himself, he looked at the bird, which kept pouring forth its mellow notes and would not cease to sing. Then Robin said:

"Now, by my faith, this night I had a dream, and it seemed to me that two strong yeomen fought with me fast and furiously. Methought they did beat me and bind me fast to a tree, taking from me both bow and arrows. If I be Robin, and am awake in this merry wood, I will take revenge on those two."

Little John, who lay by his side, had also been awakened by the song-bird and heard what Robin said.

"Dreams are swift, master," quoth he, "even as the wind that blows o'er the hill. For if it be never so loud this night, to-morrow, none the less, it may be still enough."

"Marry, that is truth," quoth Robin, "but I shall go to seek yonder strong yeomen, if in the forest they be."

ROBIN HOOD

So he leaped up, and, throwing off his covering, shouted to his comrades: "My merry men, bestir yourselves, and all make ready. Little John, thou shalt go with me."

So they all cast off their cloaks, took up their bows, and, after partaking of a hearty breakfast, stood ready to march wherever their brave captain should direct. And a fine body of men they were—alert, strong, brave, obedient—so Robin and Little John thought, as they strode past in single file away to the green forest.

By the time the sun had risen high in all his glorious splendor, the little birds were singing on every spray and twig; the cool morning air was just crisp enough to make walking in the fair forest a delight and put all in a joyous mood. The band had struck a different path under the leadership of Will Scarlet, though ever within sound of Robin's bugle-call as he strode along by the side of Little John. Anon the two came in sight of a tall figure leaning against a tree. He had a long sword and two sharp daggers that he wore by his side, and his body was covered with the hide of a horse, ears, mane, and tail complete.

"God-a-mercy," said Robin, "what is this thing? Is it man or beast?"

"Stand still," quoth Little John, "under this greenwood tree while I go forth to yon strange thing to know what it doth mean."

"Ah, John," quoth Robin, "I see well thou settest no store by me. When was I ever wont to send my men before and tarry myself behind? Were it not for the breaking of my bow, John, I would break thy head."

These words rankled harshly in John's breast. He spake not a word in answer, but turned aside with tears in his eyes, and then strode swiftly away to join the main band, leaving Robin standing silent, alone.

He had gone but a short distance when he heard sounds. As he hurried forward, the sounds became shouts and cries, and at last, when he came near, he beheld a full pitched battle 'twixt the outlaw band and the Sheriff's men. As he rushed along his heart grew sick with heaviness, for he saw two of the band lying dead in a hollow piece of ground by the side of a glade,

ROBIN HOOD

and in the distance was Will Scarlet, leaping along over rocks and stones for his very life, with the Sheriff and seven score of his men close at his heels.

"One shot now I will shoot," quoth John, "with all my might and main to make yon Sheriff that presses on so fast stop in his career."

Then he bent his great long-bow and pulled so hard that it burst in twain and the parts fell down at his feet.

"Woe is me," he cried, "thou wicked wood, that ever thou didst grow on a tree; for now this day I am undone when I need thee most."

The arrow flew, but with such a bad aim that instead of hitting the Sheriff it struck Will-a-Trent to the ground—one of the Sheriff's men who was very friendly to the band. Little John's heart was crushed, and his hands hung limp by his side. Heedless of all that was going on in the fight, he was caught by a number of the Sheriff's men, who took him and quickly bound him to a tree.

When the Sheriff heard that Little John was taken, he came up to where the outlaw was pinioned, to jeer and mock at him. "I have thee now," snarled he. "Thou shalt be drawn uphill and down dale tied to a horse's tail. Then I will hang thee on the topmost tower of Nottingham Castle."

"Yet," quoth Little John, unafraid, "thou mayst fail of thy purpose, if the good saints have their will. Our men are not all in my case."

"No," roared the Sheriff, "but Robin Hood is now in the toils of the brave Sir Guy of Gisbourne."

Little John knew of this fell knight, and his heart sank lower than ever to think that Robin was left alone with this villain, whom he now knew to be the creature standing by the tree. So he repented sore that he had crossed his dear master and had left him to his fate.

So soon as Little John was gone, Robin Hood marched up to the man in the horse-hide robe.

"Good morrow, good fellow!" quoth he.

ROBIN HOOD

"Good morrow, good fellow, to thee," the other made answer.

"Methinks by that bow thou dost bear in thy hand thou shouldst be a fair archer," said Robin.

"I have lost my way," said the stranger, "and know not where to go."

"I'll lead thee, good fellow, through the forest and be thy guide," quoth Robin.

"I am seeking for an outlaw," the stranger went on, "that men call Robin Hood, and I would give forty pounds if I could meet with him here."

"Then come along with me, bold fellow, and Robin thou shalt soon see. But first, under this greenwood tree let us test each other's skill with bow and shaft, for haply we may meet this Robin Hood by some odd chance in the mean time."

"I like thy plan, brave archer," said the stranger; and forthwith they cut a thin sapling that grew among the underbrush, which they set in the ground, with a little garland on the top, threescore rods away.

"Lead on, good fellow," quoth Robin, "and shoot, I prithee."

"Nay, by my faith, good fellow," said the other, "thou shalt shoot first."

"Well, so be it," quoth Robin; "I will even do as thou sayest." The first time Robin shot he missed the wand by an inch; and the stranger, though a right good archer, shot a foot or more away. But upon the second trial he placed the arrow inside the garland. Then Robin, as he had done many times before, loosed a shaft that cut the wand in twain.

"A blessing upon thy heart," said the stranger. "Fellow, thy shooting is good; and if thy heart be as good as thy hand, Robin Hood could do no better. Now tell me thy name, brave archer."

"Nay, by my faith," quoth bold Robin, "that will I not tell till thou hast told me thine."

"I dwell," said he, "upon the moorlands of Yorkshire, and when I am called by my right name, men call me Sir Guy of Gisbourne."

"My dwelling," slowly said Robin, "is in this very wood, and men know me as Robin Hood."

ROBIN HOOD

Then, with his hand upon the hilt of his sword, Sir Guy roared out: "Thou art he whom I have long sought."

"Well," quoth Robin, "I am ready, and care naught for thee. Prepare thyself, for with my good broadsword will I cut short thy evil day."

Robin drew his sword, and Sir Guy his, at the same time unsheathing his long, pointed Irish dagger, which he held in his left hand. Facing each other with keen eyes, they watched their chance. Both knew the combat was to be long and fierce; both were equally determined to win. Each found the other a worthy foe, for in skill and hardihood they were well matched. No one was by to see fair play, save the little birds, and they were soon scared away by the noise of the clashing swords and the deep, angry oaths of the fell Sir Guy, as he fiercely lunged, parried, and feinted. Robin was well aware of the peril in which he stood. Sir Guy was fighting for a great prize. The victor would live, the vanquished would surely die. It was a grim battle to the death.

Two hours passed. Weary, yet still fighting, the face of Sir Guy changed from a sickly yellow to a livid blue; then, as the fight went on, his blood grew hotter and flowed to his face, darkening the color to a deep purple. His long black locks were clotted and damp with sweat, and from time to time, at each furious lunge, he swore dreadful oaths because he could not budge his pale-faced, dogged foeman. Never before in all his life did Robin fight so desperately; never before was he so near death—and he knew it. Early in the fight a faintness fell upon him; but he grimly set his teeth, and new strength came. His strokes, though they dealt no wounds, began to tell upon Sir Guy, robed as he was in a hot skin. For all his wickedness, Sir Guy was a bold warrior, as many had found to their cost, and he was too proud to ask for a moment's time to rest. Robin watched him every second, fighting carefully for fear of some false, dishonorable stroke, for he knew that he had to do with a man who would not scruple to kill him by foul means.

All of a sudden Robin slipped on a root, falling on one knee. Sir Guy sprang forward nimbly and struck him in the left side

ROBIN DROVE HIS BLADE THROUGH SIR GUY'S BODY

ROBIN HOOD

—a base and cowardly deed, for a true knight would have lowered his blade till his foe got upon his feet.

"By our dear Lady," cried Robin, " 'tis not a good man's destiny to die before his day. Take that, thou villainous cheat!" So saying, he leaped up and straightway, with a sudden stroke, drove his blade right through Sir Guy's body. The knight fell backward, his sword dropped from his uplifted arm, and he slowly sank lifeless to the sward.

"There is now an end to one who hath been a traitor all his life," quoth Robin, as he leaned panting upon his sword. "Lie there, Sir Guy! If thou hadst fought as befitted a knight, mayhap thou wouldst now be alive, and I lying there in thy stead. But now thy knavishness hath undone thee, and truly the world is well rid of thee."

Robin's wound was but a scratch, for he had partly turned the blow. When he had bound it up and rested a little, he doffed his coat of Lincoln green, and clad himself from top to toe in the horse-hide, saying, "Now I will see how my men have fared and what hath befallen Little John." Anon he put Sir Guy's horn to his lips and blew so loud a blast that the Sheriff heard it as he stood upon a little hill waiting for the welcome sound.

"Hearken," quoth the Sheriff, "for I hear good tidings. Yonder I hear Sir Guy blowing his horn, as he said he would do when he had slain Robin Hood. Ay, by the mass, yonder comes the good knight, clad in his horse-hide coat. Come hither, come hither to me, thou good Sir Guy. Ask whatever thou wilt of me!"

"Oh, I will have none of thy gold," said Robin, "nor do I crave any reward save only this: now that I have slain the master, let me go and strike down the knavish servant at yonder tree. None other fee will I have."

"Thou art a madman," said the Sheriff, "and art truly unworthy of a knight's fee." But he pressed him no further, thinking so large a sum were as well in his own pocket. So he granted Robin's request, though in his heart he longed to carry Little John back to Nottingham alive, as his own prisoner.

When Little John heard his master's voice he knew his freedom was close at hand through some good hap, and now he saw Robin coming as fast as he could hie to cut his bonds. The Sheriff and his men followed close upon Robin's heels to witness the end of Little John.

"Stand aback, stand aback," shouted Robin. "Why do ye draw so near? It is not the custom in my country for more than one to hear a man's last confession. Put some space between us, while I do this deed."

So the men backed away; and Robin, pulling forth the Irish knife, quickly loosed the bonds that held Little John's hands and feet. Then, giving him Sir Guy's bow and arrows, he bade him look to himself. Both turned about at the same instant with bows ready bent; and when the Sheriff saw that his prisoner was free, he knew that Robin Hood had again foiled his plans. The shock was so great that he had no heart to stand and brave it out, but turned aside and made him ready in all haste to ride toward his home in Nottingham town. He fled full fast, and all his company did likewise, for they knew the deadly aim of those two archers who had so just a cause for anger against them. But before the Sheriff could ride out of sight Little John shot an arrow which wounded him in the shoulder. Thus he rode into Nottingham town with the broad arrow sticking from his back.

Then it was that Little John turned to Robin, saying: "My dear, good master, I do freely ask thy pardon, and shouldst thou grant it me I make a vow nevermore to cross thy will or leave thee again in the lurch."

"Nay, nay, my trusty John, my best of true hearts, 'tis I should ask pardon of thee, for I was out of temper and hasty of speech, so that I spake unkindly."

Thereupon they embraced and kissed each other full fondly on either cheek and wept. Then through the forest these two firm friends of over a quarter of a century strode together, in quiet happiness, back home to their trysting-place, where they found most of their comrades safe and happy. So the night was spent in feasting and tales of deeds nobly done on that famous day when Sir Guy of Gisbourne was slain.

XVIII

ROBIN RESCUES WILL STUTELY

ON the following morning the outlaws began to be anxious because one of their comrades had not yet joined them. This was Will Stutely—a stout yeoman, and a cousin of Robin's, whom he loved well. Those who saw him last, as they fought side by side against the Sheriff's men, said that he was running with all speed, followed by a dozen of his enemies. But they thought that Will would easily escape, because of his well-known fleetness of foot and his thorough knowledge of the forest paths. Quoth Robin:

"My dear cousin I must not lose. Therefore without more ado we will go to search for him."

At that very moment they saw a town spy come running up with great speed.

"Tidings, brave Robin Hood," cried he, "ill tidings do I bring of Will Stutely."

"What are thy tidings, trusty spy?" said Robin Hood. "Speak, I beseech thee."

"Thy cousin Will was surprised by three of the Sheriff's men, and now he lies in the dungeon of Nottingham Castle, whence he will be taken belike to-morrow, to be hanged from a cart gibbet in the public square, outside the walls. But before they could place him in the dungeon he did slay two of those that set upon him, which made the Sheriff so angry that he fain would hurry him to the gallows."

When Robin heard this dismal news he was sorely grieved, and he swore a great oath that Will Stutely should be rescued, though many a gallant yeoman should die for his sake.

Straightway they made ready to go and storm the castle in Nottingham. When the whole band stood all in a row, dressed in Lincoln green, with stout yew bows at their backs and broadswords hanging at their sides, they made a gallant show. As for Robin, he was clad from top to toe in scarlet. No braver sight could be seen in all the world on this bright, early morning, as they marched along the well-known paths, firmly resolved to bring Will Stutely back home, or die in the attempt. At the skirts of the forest the people saw them striding along fully armed, with set faces, and they knew there would be lively doings that day in Nottingham town. Many a cheer went up from yeoman throats, for all knew of Will Stutely's capture. Such news sped like wildfire o'er the town.

When the band drew near the castle, Robin Hood bade them stand. "I hold it good," said he, "that we stay here in ambush, and send forth one to find out at what time the hanging is to be. Do thou, good Friar Tuck, go forth to yonder palmer that stands beside the castle wall. Some news he may tell to thee."

With that, stepped forth bold Friar Tuck, and thus spake to the old man:

"I pray thee, aged palmer, tell me, if thou dost know, when Will Stutely must die—he that is of bold Robin Hood's men and now lies in the dungeon."

"Alack the day!" said the palmer, "Will Stutely must be hanged this day upon the gallows. O that his noble master did know! He would surely send some of his bold outlaws to succor the young man, and take him away from so vile a death."

"Ay, that is true," quoth Friar Tuck, "most truly would they

WILL STUTELY

ROBIN HOOD

soon set him free if they were near this place. But fare thee
well, thou good old man, farewell and many thanks for thy
news. If Will Stutely is hanged this day, be sure his death will
be bitterly revenged; for I must tell thee that Robin Hood is
aware of the Sheriff's order."

The Friar was no sooner gone away from the palmer than the
great castle gates were opened wide, and there Will Stutely
stood, bound in a cart drawn by a black horse, guarded on
every side. The rope dangled above his head, and the sturdy
hangman sat beside the captive. As the cart moved outside
the castle gate Will looked about to see if no help were nigh.
Then he spake boldly to the Sheriff:

"Now I see that I needs must die, yet grant me one boon, for
my noble master never had a man that was hanged upon a tree.
Give me a sword in my hand, I pray, and unbind my thongs,
that I may die bravely fighting either with thee or thy men.
I will fight till I lie dead on the ground, or, if ye are such cowards
that ye dare not meet me in fair fight, let me kill myself."

But the Sheriff was deaf to his pleadings, for he had sworn
the outlaw should be hanged, and not killed as a brave man.

"Do thou, Sheriff, but unbind my hands, I implore," again
cried Will. "I ask not now to fight, but only to slay myself,
that I may not disgrace my comrades."

"Oh, no, not so," the Sheriff said. "Thou shalt surely die on
the gallows like a dog hung up by the neck, and so shall thy
master, too, if ever he comes into my power."

Then cried Will scornfully: "Thou dastardly villain! Thou
faint-hearted peasant slave! If ever my master should cross
thy path after this foul deed he will serve thee as thou servest
me. Mark that, Sheriff, thou shalt yet hang from a tree."
With yet bolder words he went on: "My noble master scorneth
such a vile thing as thou and all thy cowardly crew, who are
too faint-hearted to subdue a man so brave. Do your worst;
I defy such wretches, and will show you how a brave man can
meet death, however it come."

To all this the Sheriff made no answer. To say sooth, he was

ROBIN HOOD

thinking deeply if this bold young man's word might perchance come true.

Then all was quiet as they drove along to the gallows, and Will closed his eyes to murmur to himself a silent prayer. When he again looked about him he saw the long form of Little John leap forward out of some bushes and quickly run up to him, crying:

"I pray thee, Will, before thou diest, bid us farewell and take leave of all thy good friends." Then, turning to the soldiers on guard, quoth John: "I must needs borrow this young man for a little. How say you, good Sheriff?"

"Now, as I live," the Sheriff bawled out, in great anger, "that long-legged varlet must be some sturdy rebel to act thus boldly to my face in defiance of the law. Seize him, guards, and see that ye hold him fast."

But Little John leaped nimbly into the cart and hastily cut Will Stutely's bonds. Then in a trice he snatched a sword from one of the Sheriff's men, saying, "Here, Will, take thou this good blade. Use it as well as thou mayst. Aid will come to thee straightway." Both turned back to back, bidding a bold defiance to all, and shouted loudly, "Robin Hood and his merry men have come to the rescue."

Straightway Robin and all his brave archers appeared, with shafts ready nocked to let fly at the word of command. Robin stood with his long arrow pointed straight at the breast of the Sheriff, who saw with dismay that he was once more befooled and that his life was not worth a straw. With trembling voice he cried to his men:

"Make haste, let us begone, for our lives are in danger." Then he put spurs to his horse, which ran with might and main back to town. When they saw their master flee, his doughty men soon followed in his path.

"Oh, stay, oh, stay awhile!" cried Will Stutely. "Run not so fast away, but take leave of us ere you go. Here is Robin Hood now, that you were so fain to hang." Then, turning to Robin and his men, he said: "Ah, my dear comrades, I little

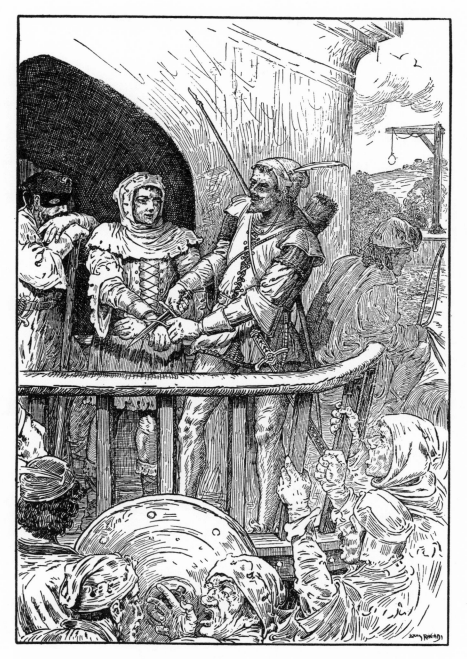

LITTLE JOHN HASTILY CUT WILL STUTELY'S BONDS

ROBIN HOOD

thought as I stood in that cart to have seen the face of my dear master and Little John again, because I knew not how to send tidings of my ill luck."

Thus it was that Will Stutely was set free without the shedding of a single drop of blood or the shooting of a single arrow.

Their mission being fulfilled, they all turned to march quietly back to the forest, having no will for revenge or pillage. As for Will, he was little the worse for his adventure, and the band were well satisfied to get him back so easily and without scathe. Full joyously they feasted, that night, under the great oak, while the Sheriff was filled with bitter shame when he found himself seated at his table with the many guests he had bidden to witness the hanging of the outlaw.

XIX

ROBIN AND SIR RICHARD O' THE LEA

TO hearty bodies and active minds feasting and merriment are but passing pleasures. A few days after Will Stutely was rescued Robin's merry men found the time hanging heavily upon their hands. The larder was well filled, and they pined for something to do. As for Robin, his last fierce combat with Sir Guy had given him his fill of fighting; and, moreover, he knew that to follow up his victory over the Sheriff past a certain point would only bring disaster. If the Sheriff let him be, he would do the same by the Sheriff. He had no wish to be driven from a place made comfortable after so many years of labor, and he was well aware that a trained band of brave soldiers under a capable leader could bring ruin to his forest kingdom. So he wisely let well alone and made up his mind to enjoy the good things he had.

One fine May day as he stood leaning against a tree, Little John, Will Scarlet, and Friar Tuck came and stood beside him. It was at the noon-hour, and Little John said to him:

"Master, let us now go to dine."

Then spake good Robin. "To eat I have no will, till I have

some stranger-guest to dine with me. Perchance if thou goest to the highway, thou mayst bring in some fat bishop, abbot, or knight dwelling hereabouts who would be willing to pay for his feast."

Quoth Little John: "Master, before we go to search for a guest, tell unto us thy desire. Whom shall we take? Whom shall we leave, and where shall we abide? Whom shall we beat and bind, and whom let go without hurt?"

"We have no foes," quoth Robin, "that do us hurt. Look to it ye do no harm to any husbandman that tilleth with his plow, for he works to our good and the weal of merry England. Likewise, harm not good yeomen or craftsmen, for they, too, must work in peace for the general good. Marry, an you meet by the way any knight or squire that would be good fellows, urge them to be with me and share our cheer. But those proud and lofty bishops and archbishops that by craft and guile extort their ill-gotten gains from the thrifty poor, beat them and bind them and bring them hither, for they are ever ready to eat and take their fill of good things. And above all, bear in mind the High Sheriff of Nottingham, who has tasted our good cheer so oft. Let him know that he is still welcome."

"We shall bear in mind thy commands, good master," said Little John, "and the lesson take to heart."

"It is a fair day," quoth Robin. "God send us a guest, that we may together enjoy a merry feast! Take thy good bow in hand. Let Will Scarlet and our holy friar wend with thee as comrades. Then walk up Ermine Street, there to wait for some willing guest that by chance may pass that way. Be he earl or baron, abbot or knight, bring him to lodge with me."

So away strode the three companions through the forest glade, and in due time they got upon the broad highway of Ermine Street, one of the five great roads of England. They looked eastward and westward, but nobody of the sort they awaited chanced to pass by. Yet after a little while, on looking up a small side lane, they beheld a knight riding slowly toward them. Stepping forth to meet him, they saw that he seemed sad and dreary, without any pride in himself. One foot was in a stirrup, the other hung outside. His hood had fallen awry, and his clothes were simple and poor. Indeed, a more doleful-seeming knight they had never looked upon. Stepping forward, Little John bent his knee, saying:

"Welcome to thee, gentle knight. Welcome be thou to our greenwood. My master hath bidden thee to a merry feast, courteous sir. We three are sent to bring thee to it."

"Who is your master?" said the knight.

Quoth John, "He is bold Robin Hood."

"He is a good yeoman," replied the knight. "And I hear naught but good of him. Therefore I do grant your request, and with you, my brethren, will wend, though my purpose was to have dined this day at Blythe or Doncaster." The gentle knight then rode along with the outlaws; and, as they wended their way, ever and anon tears ran down his cheeks. Much they marveled what it could be that made the knight so unhappy. Soon they reached the great oak, where Robin stood ready to receive them. Raising his cap, he bent his knee, saying: "Welcome, Sir Knight, thou art to me. I have been fasting, gentle sir, for three hours till thou shouldst come to us."

Then, with words fair and free, the gentle knight made answer:

"God save thee, Robin Hood, and all thy brave companions."

"Grammercy, Sir Knight. Let us together go to wash, for the feast is even now spread."

The sad knight was placed betwixt Robin and John, and he marveled at the good things laid before him. Bread and wine there were in plenty—the choicest cuts of venison, swans, pheasants, and capons—indeed, no game or bird good for eating was lacking at the board. "Eat heartily, sir knight," quoth Robin, "for our store is full."

"Grammercy, sir," said the knight. "Such a dinner I have not seen these many weeks, and should I come again to these parts, I hope to make a feast as fine for thee."

"In truth," said Robin, "I was never so greedy as to crave a return for my entertainment. I know it is not the custom

Sir Richard O' the Lea

for a yeoman to provide for a knight, but whether thou payest or not before thou dost go hence, I care not."

"I have not now the means to pay thee, good Robin, for I have naught in my purse—to my very shame be it said. Could I but do so, I would gladly pay for thy hearty fare, but of a truth there is naught in my purse save a scurvy ten shillings— an unworthy sum to offer thee."

"If that be the truth, an thou hast no more," said Robin, "I will not take a penny of it. Go forth now, Little John, and tell me the truth. If there be no more than ten shillings in the knight's purse, not one penny will I touch."

Then Little John went and took the purse that hung from the saddle of the knight's horse, and, laying his mantle on the ground, shook out the coins upon it. Letting the money lie there, he went back to his master, saying:

"The knight hath spoken the truth. There were but ten shillings in the purse."

"Fill up a cup of the best wine," quoth Robin, "and the knight shall drink to better times! No marvel his raiment is so poor, since his purse is so thin." For in sooth he was filled with pity to see a knight without means to support his high station. "Tell me one word," he said to the knight. "I trow thou wert made a knight perforce, without money at hand to uphold it, or, peradventure, thou hast lost thy goods and lands by sorry husbandry, living at strife with thy neighbors."

"By our Good Lady," said the knight, "none of these things is true, for my ancestors have been knights more than a hundred years, with lands and castles of their own, bringing in good revenue. But sometimes, Robin, it may befall a man to have trouble, and even disgrace; yet God, in His good time, doth amend his state. I am known as Sir Richard o' the Lea, and, as my neighbors will tell thee, till two or three years agone I had four hundred pounds of good money to spend as I would. But now I have, I fear, neither lands nor goods. All is lost to me save my wife and children. To this sad state have I been

ROBIN HOOD

brought, not by mine own doings, but in such a way that I could not help it."

"In what manner hast thou lost thy riches and lands?" asked Robin.

With tears in his eyes, the knight replied: "For my great folly—so men say—and for the great love I bear to my dear son, that should have been my heir. When he was twenty years old he was ever eager to joust in the tournaments, for he was brave and bold; and in a quarrel he chanced to slay a knight of Lancashire. Thus, to save him in his rights, I was fain to sell all my goods and chattels, and pledge my lands until a certain day to the rich Prior of Saint Mary's Abbey."

"What is the amount to which thou art bound?" said Robin. "Come, tell me the exact sum."

"The sum is a large one—four hundred pounds, to a shilling."

"And now, having leased thy lands," said Robin, "what shall befall thee? What canst thou do now?"

"All I can do," replied Sir Richard, "is to place my children and dear wife in the care of some good abbess and go to the wars over the salt sea, perchance to mend my sad state. So now, fare thee well, good friend, and have good day." Bitter tears trickled down from his eyes, and he could speak no more for a space. "One parting word, my merry and kind friends," he said, at last: "perchance a time may come when I shall have money to pay."

"Nay, tarry awhile," quoth Robin. "Where be thy friends? Surely a worthy knight in distress can borrow or get help for a brother's love."

"Brave outlaw, knights are not all noble. Now they scarce seem to know me, though while I was rich at home they would boast loudly enough of their great love to me. They shun me, taking no more heed of my great dole than if I were a stranger."

For very pity, then, wept all the outlaws. Robin thought of his own early life—how his uncle had cheated him—and he asked himself, Why should I not help this very worthy knight? "Be of good cheer, brave knight," he said, "and fill up another cup of the good wine. Tell me, hast thou no friend who will go surety should I lend thee the sum of which thou standest in such sore need?"

"Nay, by Him that made me and shaped the sun and moon! He is the only friend to whom I can look for help—He and our Lady Dear, who hath never failed me before."

"By my faith," said Robin, "if I searched all England through, there is no better sponsor, and She shall stand surety for thee. Go forth now, Little John, to my treasury and count out four hundred pounds, and look to it thou dost count a-right, no more nor less. Then bring it to us here."

Straightway went Little John, blithe of heart, to the treasury; and Will Scarlet followed on, for both were eager to see the sad knight made happy again. So they counted out the money, but Little John was over-generous, adding a little extra.

Then said Will, "Is it counted a-right?"

"What ails thee, Will?" said John. "Are we not giving aid to help a good and true knight who hath fallen upon sad times? He will repay to our great credit. We have enough and to spare." Even so, he was not yet contented, for when he delivered the gold, he said: "Master, ye must give the knight a livery to lap up his body, for his raiment is very thin and worn. Ye have scarlet and green stuffs, and many rich garments. There is no merchant in merry England, I dare say, that hath so much."

"Give him, then," quoth Robin, "three yards of every color, and see that he getteth full measure."

John took good care of that, for he used no other measure than his long-bow, and with every yard he put in an extra piece for good luck.

"Thou wouldst ruin thy master if he were a draper," said Will, who stood by and laughed. "By my troth, John, we might as well give the knight good measure. It hath cost us little to get."

When the cloth had been brought and set before Robin and Sir Richard, Little John said:

"Thou must give the knight a horse to carry home all these

goods. Now that we have begun to help him, let us do it well."

"Ay, marry, that we will. So bring the gray courser and put on a new saddle. I can see, too, that the knight needeth a pair of boots. But in faith, dear John, since thou hast been so generous with our things, what wilt thou thyself give the good knight?"

"I shall give him, sir," quoth John, "a pair of gilt spurs, with a prayer that God may bring him soon out of his unhappy state."

Then Sir Richard wore a cheerful smile, seeing how these noble outlaws did good deeds to him, and he said to Robin:

"My loving and kind sir, when shall I return to pay this great debt I owe thee?"

"Let it be this day twelvemonth, an it please thee, Sir Knight, under this great oak tree."

So the knight made ready to depart, a great load having fallen from him since he entered the outlaws' glade. But Robin bade him tarry, saying:

"It would be a great shame for a brave knight to ride alone, without either squire, yeoman, or page by his side. In case of need to guard the money, I shall lend thee Little John to serve as yeoman for a while."

At last the knight started on his way, with Little John by his side, and as he looked back to the great oak he waved his hand and blessed Robin Hood for his great kindness. Never before had he, in any company, met with such brotherly love, and all had been done in such a way as not to hurt his pride. After he had ridden some distance the now happy knight spake to John, saying:

"To-morrow I must perforce go to the Prior of Saint Mary's Abbey in York town, to pay this four hundred pounds. If I be not there by to-morrow even, all my lands are lost to me forever. The Prior, I trow, would fain seize this land from me, for I know him to be a hard, grasping churchman."

"Have no fear, Sir Knight," quoth Little John. "I warrant we shall be there in good time. Yet we will hasten our pace and

ROBIN HOOD

push along the Trent valley due north. We can pass by Doncaster before nightfall, then with a good rest and early start we shall be in York by afternoon."

On the afternoon of the next day, the Prior of Saint Mary's Abbey was seated at his ease near a table upon which were spread luscious fruits, cakes, and wines. With him was a man of the law, whom he had summoned to draw up legal papers in case the knight failed to appear, also the Sheriff to represent the county where the land in question lay. Quoth the Prior to his abbot, as he sipped his wine:

"This day, twelvemonth agone, there came a knight to borrow four hundred pounds upon all his free lands. If he come not soon, he shall forfeit all, and the lands shall fall to Holy Church."

"It is full early," said the abbot. "The day is not yet far gone. Be patient with him a little while. I had as lief pay a hundred pounds to have you tarry till even. The knight perchance hath been far beyond the sea, and when in England once more, things will go better with him. He may have suffered both hunger and cold. Great pity 'twere to take his land, at least before his time is ended. God-a-mercy, have you no conscience, Prior Vincent, to do the knight such great harm?"

The Prior's face turned deep red with anger as he replied, "Thou hast ever some reason to urge against the gaining of more riches for the abbey, and in the guise of charity dost delight to cross me."

The man of law bade them have patience, at least till the full time was past; for, said he, "The knight may be dead or hanged, or drowned; then his lands and rents will justly fall to you."

While they were talking and waiting they heard a sound of horses' hoofs in the courtyard, and through the half-open door they saw the knight. " 'Tis he," said the Prior, with a sad face, "but mayhap he hath not the money." Then the knight dismounted, and, still wearing his poor mantle, to make the Prior think he had no money, drew nigh to the gate.

"Welcome, Sir Knight," said the porter at the door. "My

ROBIN HOOD

Lord Prior, with his men, are waiting to greet thee." Then the porter swore a great oath that never had he seen so fine a horse. "I will straightway lead him to the stable," quoth he, "and give him some fodder."

"Nay, not so," quoth the knight. "Let the horse stand where he is." So saying, he strode into the presence of the Prior and his friends. Saluting them, he knelt down, saying, "Right glad am I, Sir Prior, to come as I promised on this day."

"Well," said the Prior, in a surly tone, "hast thou brought my pay?"

Then the knight bethought him to make a test, to see whether the Prior had a hard or a merciful heart; so he said:

"Not a penny."

"Thou art a shrewd debtor," quoth the Prior. "Drink to me, Sir Sheriff, for the land is now mine." Then, addressing the knight, he said, "Wherefore dost thou come here, if indeed thou hast no money?"

"I come thus, on my knees, to pray thee that thou wilt give me a little time of grace—a few months—for I have found good friends that will then help me in my sore need."

"The time is past," quoth the man of law, "and thy land is now forfeit to the Prior."

"Nay, say not so. Be my friend and defend me, for the Prior is rich and I am poor."

But the lawyer had been promised a good fat fee, so he answered, "I hold by the Prior in his rights."

Then Sir Richard turned to the Sheriff, saying, "Take pity, Sir Sheriff, and use thy good offices in my behalf."

"Nay, in sooth," was the curt reply, "that I will not."

Again the knight besought the Prior to be merciful. "For I will be thy true servant till the four hundred pounds are fully paid."

"Nay, by the mass," sternly replied the Prior, "of this land thou wilt get none."

Then, rising from his knees and standing proudly up before them, the knight cried angrily: "By Saint Dunstan, if I do not get what is mine, full dear ye shall buy it."

"I COME TO PRAY THEE THAT THOU WILT GIVE ME A LITTLE TIME OF GRACE"

ROBIN HOOD

Straightway the Prior began to abuse him and spake evil words to him, his anger swelling ever the more as he talked. "Out upon thee, thou false, beggarly knight," he said at last; "speed thy way out of my hall."

But Sir Richard made a threatening step forward, and in a stern voice cried: "Thou liest, Prior Vincent, false knight I never was. My fame and good name are known among true hearts. In jousts and tournaments have I always been at the front, and all that know me can bear witness to my bravery and truth. No true churchman, prior or bishop, would be so discourteous as to let a noble knight kneel so long."

Then the sharp man of law perceived that, as the time was not yet past, it might be that the knight could pay. So he turned to the Prior, saying:

"What wilt thou give if the knight will release his land, for you may have some trouble to keep it in peace?"

"A hundred pounds will I give," said the Prior.

"Nay, give him two hundred," said the lawyer.

"Thou wicked Prior," quoth Sir Richard, "I vow thou shalt not be my heir, though thou givest a thousand more." Then upon the table he upturned his bag of gold. "There are thy four hundred pounds, thou wretched usurer. Hadst thou shown me any courtesy or spoken one word of kindness, some interest would have been thy reward."

When the Prior saw the gold he stood speechless with amazement, and he pushed his wine-cup away from him. Then he asked the man of law to give him back his fee, now that no deed was to be made.

"Nay, not a penny do I give back," cried the lawyer.

The Prior's face turned red with shame and anger; he lay back in his wide arm-chair, closed his eyes, and would not speak a word.

"Sir Prior," quoth the knight, "and thou man of law, now that I have paid my debt the land is mine for aught ye can gainsay."

Then he strode to the door, all his troubles over, with a bright and cheerful face. At a near-by inn he donned his best clothing, and, mounting his horse, rode away, well satisfied that he had

ROBIN HOOD

with dignity and noble demeanor shamed the wily Prior as a true knight should do. The joy he felt in being rid of his great burden and his delight in looking forward to the meeting with wife and family were unbounded. The woodland notes of songbirds, the pretty flowers and green leaves, all seemed so much more beautiful when he thought of his unhappy state before he met Robin Hood, who seemed to him the kindest and best of men. Now he was riding home as a noble knight should, with lofty mien, rich raiment, a fine horse and trappings, and a servant by his side. "Truly, my kind-hearted John," said he, "how sweet is life after bitter trials! The thanks I owe thy master and thee, I cannot now put into words."

Right on they rode until they came to Sir Richard's Castle of Briarlea. As he drew nigh to the gate his noble lady met him, saying:

"Welcome, my dear husband. Are our land and castle lost to us, or hath aught been saved?"

"Be merry, good lady," quoth the knight, "and pray for Robin Hood, that his soul may be ever in bliss. He it was that helped me in my hour of need, and were it not for his great kindness, we should now surely be beggars without home or land. The greedy Prior hath been paid, and all is now our very own." Then he told how, while on his way to ask the Prior for more time, the good Robin Hood had invited him to dine and had loaned him the money to be paid in a year.

"Now," he finished, "we will dwell peacefully at home, and with careful saving gather together the four hundred pounds ready to pay at the appointed time."

Little John stayed with the knight and did his duty well, though he pined to be back again at the oak glade. Yet he patiently waited till the twelve months passed by. Then, true to his knightly pledge, Sir Richard rode back once again to Sherwood Forest and there paid back to Robin all he owed. Amid feasts and merrymaking, Little John was welcomed home, and the knight's freedom from debt was cheered and celebrated in joyous songs.

XX

ROBIN MEETS MAID MARIAN

WHILE Little John was away at Sir Richard's castle, serving as his squire, Robin Hood and all his merry men sorely missed him. The tall outlaw was so jolly and kind of heart that every one of his companions loved him full dear. For a time the oak glade seemed dull, and Allan-a-Dale was more often asked to sing or play. Friar Tuck and Will Scarlet did their best to make Robin be of good cheer, and right glad were they when some adventure fell in their way.

With the long years of woodland life, Robin Hood had changed but little in face or form, though he had gained much in wisdom. He was more resourceful than of yore, and through constant practice with long-bow, sword, and quarter-staff, both in play and in stern battles, he was perfect master of all his men. No longer young, he was now just past the prime of life, and an extremely handsome man. His curly locks and beard of a red-brown color set off his dark, ruddy complexion. His clothes were either of deep Lincoln green or deep scarlet. Always as neat as a pin, his weapons ever in perfect order, he was looked upon as a hero by women and children when seen on the great

ROBIN HOOD

highway or at church. His manner to all, both high and low, was kind, without the slightest trace of pride or vainglory, and his charity was unbounded. If he met young lads venturing in the forest after birds' nests, or hunting small game, he would take the greatest pains to bring down some rare animal or bird for them with his unerring shaft. If he met little lassies a-black-berrying, he had ever some coins in his pouch to give them; and to the gaffers and old wives likewise he gave gifts, if need were, with kindly words to boot. Small wonder it was that the folks roundabout for miles knew him only to love and venerate him.

Now I must tell you that when Robin was a young boy living on his father's land, nigh unto Needwood Forest, in North Staffordshire, he had for a playmate a bonny maid of high degree called Maid Marian, that for rare beauty, face, and favor, no maid could excel in all the country round. To her, Robin was known as the Earl of Huntingdon, and in their childish play they pledged themselves to one another as young lovers.

But fortune severed them when Robin left his home on that fateful fifteenth birthday. Since then they had never set eyes on each other, though oft in their thoughts they loved to remember the youthful, happy days spent together. For a long time Marian was sad, and oft she sighed for her absent friend. As time went on her parents died, and she was left alone with friends, who, for a while, were kind to her because she had lands of her own. But things changed for the worse, and her lands were taken from her. Troubled in mind, she bethought her of her childhood friend, who, she heard, had become the famous outlaw, Robin Hood of Sherwood Forest. At last she made up her mind to go and seek him out, throw herself at his feet, and ask him to aid her for the sake of their old friendship. Well aware of the danger of traveling alone dressed as a woman, she decided to array herself like a youthful page and range through Sherwood Forest till she found her dear Robin Hood.

So, clad in youth's attire, with quiver and bow, sword and buckler, she started on her way, and soon reached the forest.

ROBIN HOOD

On that very same day Robin made up his mind to visit Nottingham town. To shield him from the eyes of the Sheriff and his men, he put on a patched gray suit and a hat of which he could draw the vizor down over his eyes to shade his face. He had gone some distance, and was just skirting round the wood by a well-worn but narrow pathway, when he spied a youthful form coming toward him. Making his voice deep and gruff, for fear the young stranger might be one of the Sheriff's spies, he cried out:

"What is thy business, young stranger, and where dost thou go in this wood?"

Thinking Robin was some rough thief, the youthful stranger boldly replied: "What is that to thee? I go where I list. Mind thine own affairs and leave me to mine."

"That will I not," quoth Robin. "Not one step shalt thou stir without my leave." Then, drawing his sword, he stepped forward threateningly.

But the youth drew out a thin, bright, glistening blade, and fell to with such quick blows that Robin had all he could do to guard himself.

"Thou wilt find," quoth the youth, "little though I be, that I can master thee and make some more holes in thy ragged coat—perchance in thy skin, if it be not too thick."

Robin answered not a word, but fought carefully, parrying and feinting, but striking no earnest blow, for he had no will to hurt the lad. At last the stranger, whose sword was lighter and more easily handled, gave a sudden thrust which cut a deep flesh wound across Robin's cheek, so that the blood ran fast down his face.

"Oh, hold thy hand, young sir," said Robin, in his natural voice. "Hold thy hand, and thou shalt be one of my merry men to range the forest with bold Robin Hood."

Then Marian remembered the voice of her lover, and said: "Ay, Robin, 'tis thine own self. At last I have found thee."

"In good faith, who art thou that dost remember me?"

"Why, 'tis I—Marian—the maiden friend of thy youth, come in search of thee to aid me in my sore need."

ROBIN HOOD

Then he knew that it was Marian's voice; and he drew her quickly toward him, and kissed her on the lips, like a true and loyal lover.

After a space they turned and bent their steps toward the oak glade, but on the way Marian made great dole over the wound she had given him.

"In truth," quoth jolly Robin, " 'tis naught. Right glad am I to have it, for without this wound I should not have found thee."

Anon she told him of her sorrows, and asked him if he could find a place for her safe keeping. "For, Robin," said she, "I have no other friend but thee."

"Right blithe am I that 'tis so," quoth Robin. "We will find room for thee in Allan-a-Dale's bower, under care of his wife, till the time when thou shalt set the day for Friar Tuck to marry us."

Soon they came to the oak glade, where Robin with a blast of his horn drew all his band together, and told them in few words how the case stood, and what he meant to do. Amid the loud cheers that made the woods ring and re-echo, Allan-a-Dale's wife went up to Marian and kissed her. Then, putting her arms around her waist, she led her to the bower. On that same even was such a bustling and excitement as ne'er was seen before, for all set to work in right good earnest to make a stately banquet in honor of the betrothed chief and his fair Maid Marian.

In a short space the board was set, groaning with good things. A great flagon of the best wine was placed before each man, that every one in turn might drink a merry toast to their beloved captain and his beautiful bride soon to be. When they had feasted long and well, Robin rose from the table and pledged Marian in a deep cup, after which all his tall, comely yeomen did likewise.

Thus bravely did these stout hearts wish Robin well, and each cup, as it was emptied, they filled with speed again. But all good times must have an end, and so at last their merry-making came to a close. Just as the nightingale began its sweet

ROBIN HOOD AND MARIAN IN THEIR BOWER

ROBIN HOOD

song they all went to rest, happy over the latest yet sweetest addition to their band.

'Twas not many days hence when Friar Tuck, after much thought and many whisperings with the others, announced that the wedding would now be solemnized. And so they were married, the lovely bride decked out with many beautiful jewels that were gifts from each one of the band. On this day, the great oak, as well as the whole glade, was festooned and garlanded with sweet flowers—jessamine, eglantine, honeysuckle, and wild roses, forget-me-nots from the brookside, pied daisies and cowslips. The sward was a thick carpet of sweet-smelling posies, and the merry birds, when they saw the glade turned into a garden, came to the twigs and branches and sang a glorious melody together, while the happy bride and the brave groom walked slowly, hand in hand, to their new and beautiful bower, where they lived together in great content for many a long day after.

XXI

KING RICHARD VISITS ROBIN

KING RICHARD, the mighty warrior, had now returned home to his kingdom, after an absence of more than four years in the Holy Land, fighting the Turks. A year of that time he was held a prisoner, chained in a castle in the Austrian Tyrol. He was set free upon payment of a large ransom, and finally reached England in the spring of 1194, where he met his mother, Eleanor, who told him of his brother John's rebellion. Richard at once pushed northward, and on the 28th of March the Castle of Nottingham, which was held by men-at-arms for Prince John, surrendered to the King.

The Sheriff was not slow in making complaint of the forest outlaws; and Richard, ever fond of adventure, was moved to find out for himself how the matter stood. So, much to the Sheriff's surprise, he said that he would see Sherwood Forest and meet the famous outlaw face to face.

"It is my will to go clad as monk," quoth he, "and thou shalt choose me out five knights to attend me."

"My liege," said the Sheriff, "all shall be done as thou sayest,

ROBIN HOOD

and, as ever, thou dost wisely; for a monk or prior doth never fail to entice this sly rogue."

To this King Richard answered never a word, but watched the Sheriff grimly as he made a low obeisance and departed; for, to say sooth, he loved not this wily man over well. But in what he had heard of Robin Hood and his deeds he found something to his liking. He loved not hunting the deer as his forefathers had loved it, for his great joy lay in fighting either in mortal hand-to-hand combats or in tournaments. So stark was he that no man might withstand him in single fight. None the less, he was jealous of his rights over the forests, and of the rights of his earls and barons, who might hunt as they listed so long as they gave him money and men for his wars.

Of the nine years that Richard was King of England he dwelt but nine months in his own kingdom. For the rest he was in foreign lands, either at war or as a prisoner. Like Robin Hood, he delighted to seek adventure in disguise, going oft alone, and trusting to his own courage and strength of arm.

So the day after the King came to Nottingham it was arranged that he should visit Sherwood, under the guidance of the captain of the foresters, who promised to lead him to Robin Hood's glade. King Richard was arrayed in abbot's attire, and his five knights went as monks, but all had on chain mail beneath their cloaks. Following some distance behind was the King's war-horse, fully caparisoned, together with some sumpter-horses under the care of his squires. After they had gone some distance into the deep forest it so befell that they met Robin Hood standing right in their path. Robin stepped forward and placed his hand upon the bridle of the King's horse, calling out:

"Sir Abbot, by your leave, I desire that ye abide with us awhile. We be yeomen of this forest, who live by the King's deer, for we have no other shift. But I trow thou hast many churches with rents that yield thee gold a-plenty. Therefore, good Abbot, prithee give us some of thy moneys for holy charity."

Then said the King: "Truly, I have brought with me no more than forty pounds, for I have been at Nottingham these last few days with our King, where I have spent much of my money on the great earls and barons there. Wherefore, good sir, having but forty pounds, no more can I give, though I would it were a hundred pounds that I might give unto thee."

Robin took the forty pounds, and, dividing it into parts, gave half to his men. Then he spake courteously to the abbot:

"Sir Abbot, far be it from me to take all thou hast; therefore take this other part for thine own use, and I trust we shall meet again another day."

"Grammercy," said the King. "In sooth, thou art a reasonable outlaw, and our King Richard greeteth thee, and doth send his seal to bid thee come to Nottingham, both to dine and to drink with him." Thereupon he took from his pouch the great seal, to show Robin it was in truth a royal command.

Robin uncovered his head, and knelt down on his knee, saying: "I love no man in all the world so well as I do our mighty King. Welcome, then, is this seal to me. And, Sir Abbot, for thy good tidings to-day thou shalt dine with me under my trysting-tree for the love I bear to our King."

Forthwith he led the abbot and his monks to the great oak, and, taking his horn, blew three loud blasts, whereat seven-score hardy yeomen came running, and stood ready all in a row, each man bending his knee before Robin.

The King said to himself, "Now, by Saint Austin, this to my thinking is a wonderful sight to behold; for this outlaw's men are more to his bidding than my men are to mine."

Robin then gave some orders, and straightway the yeomen hasted to make ready a feast for the King and his men. With might and main they worked, and anon before the King were set great haunches of venison and good white bread, with red wine and rich brown ale to wash it down.

"Make good cheer, Abbot," cried Robin, "and be assured that for thy tidings of the King thou art blessed in my sight. Now shalt thou see the life we lead before thou wendest thy way back to Nottingham, that thou mayst tell our brave King thereof when next thou shalt meet with him."

THE KING BEGAN TO ROLL UP HIS SLEEVE

ROBIN HOOD

When they had feasted enough, all started up in haste to show the abbot their skill with the long-bow. The King looked about him warily when he saw the outlaws bending their bows, thinking they might perchance prove traitors. But he was soon undeceived when he saw them placing two wands, with garlands of roses atop, for targets at a hundred paces away.

"The distance," quoth he, "is far too long for good aim."

Quoth Robin: "I trow that any single man who faileth to shoot through yon fair garland shall forfeit his arrows—be they made ever so fine—and, what is more, he shall get a good buffet on the head from his master."

Then each shot in turn, and those who missed Robin smote wondrous sore; for he wished the King to hear how his brave men were the best archers in merry England. In the first two rounds Robin split the wand both times, and so did Gilbert, the cook, whom they called Gilbert of the White Hands, because he was always mixing the flour to make bread. Then Little John and Will Scarlet again split the wand. At the last shot that Robin took he missed the mark full three fingers.

Then up spake good Gilbert. "Master, thine arrows are forfeit. Stand forth and take thy pay in one sound buffet."

"If it be so," quoth Robin, "I will deliver my arrows. I pray thee, Sir Abbot, to serve me well with a buffet of thy strong arm."

"It is not the custom of my order," said the King, "to smite a good yeoman, and in sooth I fear I shall do thee harm. By thy leave, good Robin, I had rather another should do it."

"I give thee leave," quoth Robin. "Smite boldly; I fear no harm from thee."

So the King, with a half-smile upon his face, began to roll up his sleeve, while Robin planted his feet wide apart and waited with a light heart, for he thought that no fat abbot would budge him. The next moment he found himself sprawling on the grass while the greenwood seemed to swim round him. Slowly he arose, rubbing his sore head.

"I make my vow," quoth he, "thou art a stalwart churchman;

ROBIN HOOD

there is pith in that tough arm of thine. No other hath e'er before smitten me so hard, and I did think that none but King Richard himself had such might of arm." Then he looked closer at the smiter, and he saw that the disguised abbot was in very truth the King. Falling again to his knee, he cried: " 'Tis my liege lord, the King of England, now I know it well. Mercy I ask, under our trysting-tree, of thy kingly goodness and grace. I ask it for all my men and for me."

"Yea, good outlaw," said the King, "thy prayer I do grant thee, on condition that thou and all thy company do forthwith leave the greenwood and come back to the court, there to dwell close to my person."

"I make my vow to God," quoth Robin, "that I will go to thy court and join thy service, and take with me my sevenscore men, to be thy loyal, true servants forevermore."

But fate decreed it otherwise, for the King went back to Nottingham to hold a great council for a judgment againt his brother, Prince John. A few weeks later he crossed from the Isle of Wight to Harfleur in France, and never returned to his court and country.

XXII

ROBIN WINS THE QUEEN'S PRIZE

 OME years after his visit to Robin Hood, King Richard went to his fathers, being wounded in the arm by an arrow shot from the bow of a young Norman, Bertrand de Gurdrum. In those days of rude surgery the barbed iron head of the shaft could not be drawn out without cruelly mangling the flesh. And so the Warrior King died. His brother, the wicked Prince John, ascended the throne and by his unwisdom lost the crown of England, the fair lands of Normandy, and other provinces. At last the barons forced him to sign the Magna Charta, after he had brought the people to a state of abject slavery. Suddenly the tyrant was called to his last account. With his army he tried to cross the estuary of the Wash against a strong inflowing tide. There the King's baggage-wagons and sumpter-horses, with his treasures, his armor, and clothing, were all swallowed up by the waters. Among them stood King John, helpless and despairing—even his crown was swept away by the strong current. Three days later he died from the exposure.

Then a little boy of nine years old became King under the name of Henry III., and at his coronation a fillet of gold was

ROBIN HOOD

placed upon his head in lieu of the crown that was lost by King John.

The young King grew to manhood, and in the course of time married Eleanor. The nuptial festivities were of extraordinary splendor. The citizens of London especially came forth with all their pomp, and among their merrymakings was a great shooting-match at which costly prizes were offered to the best archers from all over England.

Robin Hood was now past threescore and ten, though no one would take him to be more than forty-five. Breathing outdoor air night and day, living upon plain, hearty food, and practising himself in the use of all weapons as of yore, it seemed that he would always be young. There was scarce a tinge of gray in his hair or beard, and his teeth were white, glistening like those of a boy.

Little John, some years younger than Robin, was quite as hearty. Will Scarlet and the rest changed little save that the years softened and mellowed them. One or two had gone to their long rest in peace, followed by the prayers and good wishes of loving hearts. Among them had gone the good Friar Tuck, whose remains were lovingly carried through the greenwood in a huge oaken coffin, slung from the shoulders of a dozen stalwart men, to a grave beside Fountains Abbey, according to his last wish. The little chapel he had caused to be built for the especial use of the outlaws had received his careful attention to the last. Nevertheless, feeling that his time would soon come, not knowing when he might be called away, he had trained an assistant—a tall, comely lad named Cecil, whose gentleness and sweet nature filled in a measure the void left by the loss of the worthy friar. And so young Friar Cecil now called with a little bell the outlaws to vespers and matin-song.

We must now go into Nottingham town, to the Blue Boar Inn, the same place where Robin, many years ago, had befooled the Tinker and stolen his warrant. The old inn was much as before. On the same seat, at the same bench, was seated a great, tall fellow dressed in green, his long-bow and quiver at his back,

ROBIN HOOD

talking quietly to another bold archer dressed in red. Each had a tankard of ale beside him, and their looks were bent upon a handsome boy of sixteen, richly dressed as a page. The youth had just dismounted from a beautiful white steed, which he turned over to the hostler to be fed. Striding up to a bench near the archers, he called for the landlord, bidding him bring a bottle of Rhenish wine. "I pray you, brave archers," he cried, "drink me a toast to our noble and beautiful Queen Eleanor, and to my search for the bold Robin Hood."

The tall archer said to his companion, "We can drink to the first part of that, but what would he with our captain?" So they drank with the youth, and the tall fellow said: "Tell me truly what is thine errand with Robin Hood, my fair young stranger? Perchance we may guide thee to him if thou meanest no harm."

"Nay, in sooth it is not so," quoth the youth. "I tell thee truly, I am Richard Patrington, the Queen's page; and she did call me to her chamber, saying, 'Post thou to Nottingham as fast as thou canst ride; search throughout the forest of Sherwood to inquire of one good yeoman or another where Robin Hood doth abide.' "

"Tell me, sweet page," said the archer, "what is the cause that the good Queen seeketh Robin Hood?"

"Sir archer," said the page, " 'tis a message from our Queen for Robin Hood. She will have him go up to London, and will guard him from all harm, but more I will not tell thee as at this time."

"We will guide thee, young page, so mount thy white steed and follow us on through the forest."

Straightway they set out, an archer on either side of the white horse. Striding swiftly along, they reached the glade, where the band were seated or lying at ease upon the greensward.

"What gay young spark is this," cried one, "that Little John and Will Scarlet have brought unto us?" For the page was dressed in bright-colored velvets and adorned with silk ribbons and jewels.

ROBIN HOOD

"There standeth Robin Hood," quoth Little John to the page.

Thereat young Patrington stepped forward and fell on one knee, saying: "Famous outlaw, our noble Queen Eleanor doth send thee greetings by me. Having heard of thy fame as an archer, she would fain see thee and witness thy wondrous skill with the bow. Be it known to thee that our gracious King Henry of great renown will shortly hold a shooting-match in Finsbury Field, in presence of all the Court. All the best archers in merry England will strive for a grand prize, and our Queen would fain see the gallant Robin Hood the victor in the match. She bids me command thee to be present, and doth promise to guard thee and thy men that ye may return to Sherwood without harm. This gold ring is a sign of her good-will, and she biddeth thee post to fair London without any fear."

Then Robin answered: "Fair young page, I will do the commands of our noble Queen right merrily. This ring she sends by thee shall never part from me." So saying, he kissed the ring right loyally and placed it upon his finger. "Before we go, my gallant page, thou must rest and take food, the while we go to array ourselves in seemly guise." So he called Little John, Will Scarlet, and Allan-a-Dale, to go with him to the Court.

Anon they came forth, ready to start. Robin was clad from head to foot in scarlet, and his men in Lincoln green, with black caps and long, white, feathery plumes. Each had a fine horse, and with young Patrington they rode away to London town.

Early on the morn of the third day they came in sight of the walls and battlements of the city. Their young guide was of great aid in picking the way through the maze of people gathered together for this great occasion, and they soon arrived at the Court, where Queen Eleanor received Robin and his companions with much kindness.

Quoth the Queen: "Thou art welcome, bold Robin Hood, and so are thy true companions. I know of thy skill, and fear not to wager that thou wilt bear off the great prize. Go forth and do thy best."

YE GOOD
QUEEN ELEANOR

ROBIN HOOD

Then Robin kneeled, saying: "Ay, that will I, your gracious Majesty."

So on the next day there were gathered together the most famous archers of merry England at the archery range—Tepus, the bow-bearer to the King, a great favorite with the common people; also young Clifton, the winner of many prizes; and Gilbert the Smith, with his strong arm, who pulled a mighty long-bow, though in truth he was more famed for shooting far than for skill in marksmanship.

Finsbury Field was a gay sight with its throngs of people, for twenty renowned archers were about to strive for great prizes—three hundred tuns of Rhenish wine, three hundred tuns of beer, and leave to shoot three hundred of the fatted hart in Dalton Forest.

On each side of the archery range were rows and rows of seats, all filling with a noisy, chattering crowd of high officials, barons, and knights, with their ladies fair.

The targets were all set forth and the distance measured. All was in readiness, waiting the advent of the King and the Queen to take their seats on the royal dais. Soon loud cheers proclaimed their coming, and at last the trumpet sounded as the royal pair rode along with waving plumes and jewels flashing in the sunlight. Then, dismounting, they took their seats, amidst the clamorous cheers of the people.

When all were silent again, a herald entered the ground and gave three loud blasts from a silver trumpet, calling the archers before the King, to make their reverences to him before the shooting began.

Now the King was exceeding proud of the archers of his guard. He looked them over with an approving eye, well assured that he knew who would win. Oft before had these famous bowmen given him good cause for his trust; and now in right kingly, courteous fashion he bade them do their uttermost.

Amid a breathless silence the shooting began in good earnest, and soon the targets were pricked full of arrows. Upon the second trial many archers dropped out. New targets were set up, while the crowd waited impatiently to cheer and shout for their favorites.

'Twas then the noble Queen Eleanor turned to the King and asked: "Are these in truth the very best archers in merry England?"

"In good sooth," quoth the King, "not only the best in England, but in all the world besides. Who can show such skill as Gilbert, who hath twice pricked the very center with his shaft—or the bold young Clifton? Fain would I see any that could match them."

"Yet I know," replied the Queen, "of two archers who could easily better their best."

"Bring them forth, my Queen, if they be nigh," quoth the King, laughing. "With so fair a champion, they should at least do something to cover thy fair face from shame at their sure defeat."

"Of that," said Eleanor, "I have no fear, and will match two archers against all that are here to-day—providing thou, my King, wilt grant them freedom to come and go as they list."

"In sooth," laughed the King, "my fair Queen shall not ask in vain. Bring forth whatsoever archer thou wilt, and I will promise him freedom to go and come for forty days, without harm or hindrance, under thy fair favor. What is more, should any shoot better than my good bow-bearer, Tepus—or even do as well—I will give him prizes to boot. And with thee I lay a wager of a silver bugle and a gold-tipped arrow."

"I take thy wager, Harry, my King." Then, with merry laughter from all the knights and ladies near by, the Queen cried, "Is there no noble knight of our Court that will share in this wager of his Queen? Come hither to me, Sir Cyril Leigh, that art a full good knight, or thou, good Bishop of Hereford, and lay a wager upon mine archers."

"Nay, pardon, most gracious and fair Queen," quoth the Bishop, "I fear to wager what little I have against such brave archers as the King's, and I know not any strange archer that can win."

"Bring forth thy archers," said the King.

ROBIN HOOD

"Marry, I will," quoth the Queen, merrily, trusting full well that Robin would win the prize.

Then she beckoned to young Richard Patrington, and bade him call Robin Hood, who waited close by. Anon Robin and Little John were seen marching across to the Royal pavilion, where they stopped, bent their knees, and doffed their caps.

King Henry gazed for a while and was silent. When the Bishop of Hereford saw who the new-comers were, his face changed.

"By the mass," quoth he, " 'tis the saucy villain, Robin Hood, and his twin rogue, Little John," and he began to puff out with rage. But the Queen stopped his further speech with a wave of her fair hand, saying:

"My brave archers, I have laid a wager that ye will outshoot the best man now on Finsbury Field. Will ye both do your utmost to win the prize, for the sake of your Queen?"

"Ay, that we will, gracious Majesty," quoth Robin. Then catching sight of the Bishop, he said: "My gracious Queen, I would fain crave a boon of thee, which is only that I might speak a few words to my lord the Bishop of Hereford here in this presence." As he said this he quaked inwardly, despite his boldness, for the King looked black. But Queen Eleanor was in a merry mood, and thought to have some sport with the Bishop, so she said:

"Thy boon is granted."

Then Robin said unto the Bishop: "My Lord Bishop, seeing that we have known each other of old time, I make bold to ask thee what thou wilt wager with me that I have the worse in this match."

"By my silver miter," quoth the Bishop, wrathfully, "all the money within my purse, and that is fifteenscore nobles, nigh a hundred pounds." With that, he cast his purse down before Robin. Then Robin took the money pouch from his side and cast it beside the Bishop's purse.

"I know who this money must win," quoth Little John, smiling, as they went to take their places for the shooting.

As the archers were making ready for the second bout the

ROBIN HOOD

King turned to the Bishop and asked, "What is this that thou sayest? Who are these men our Queen doth champion against the flower of English archery?"

"My gracious King," quoth the Bishop, in slow, severe tones, "yon villain in red is a notorious outlaw thief from Sherwood Forest, named Robin Hood. The big, long-legged rogue in green is t'other villain's right-hand helper, whom they call Little John. Both of them took me, late one Saturday night, bound me fast to a tree, and made me sing a mass. A murrain upon him and his vile outlaw band! Many a time hath he robbed me and the Church, God wot!"

At this the King was very wroth, and his brow grew dark. Turning to the Queen, he said, in angered tones, "Can this be true?"

"What the Bishop saith," replied the Queen, "may be true; report hath it that he once made merry with Robin Hood. But remember thy royal promise of safety to those men for forty days."

"True," said the King. "The promise shall be kept, but let them beware what they do both now and when their time is past."

Then he called forth his archers and bade them sternly to redouble their efforts, because the Queen had laid a wager on the outlaw Robin Hood. "So take heed," quoth he, "that your shafts fly true and to the mark."

Now, the King's archers, like everybody else, had heard of Robin Hood; and Tepus, like a sensible man, replied simply:

"We will do our best to uphold the honor of our illustrious King."

"Well said, good Tepus. I am content, and by Saint Hubert, I believe we have the victors upon our side."

Finsbury Field was all agog with excitement, and a loud buzzing could be heard as the news spread from one to another that the great outlaw would now shoot on the Queen's wager against the King. Many in the crowd liked it not, and there were some who murmured; yet on second thought they considered

ROBIN HOOD

that it would be wiser not openly to affront the Queen, who was very popular.

The trials had now brought down the competitors to six archers for the King and only two for the Queen. The King's men were Gilbert of Warwick, stout Tepus, the bow-bearer, young Clifton of Kent, Kenneth of Tittenson, and two brothers, Hugh and Steve of the moorlands. Then came Little John and Robin Hood for the Queen.

Clad in bright colors, the men made a brave show; and so thought the people as they stretched their necks, tier above tier, to see them. Attendants had already set new targets in place, while six upright willow wands, straight and true, exactly covered the center of each target. Such a mark none was expected to touch at so long a range. A score of new long-bows lay on the ground, ready for any who should by accident damage his own weapon.

The King's archers tossed up a penny for choice of targets, but Robin and John put aside their chance, saying that all marks were the same to them. In like manner did they choose to give others the first trial. Each archer shot six arrows in turn. Tepus, leading, did well, for every arrow hung on his target. Likewise, so did Gilbert, one of his shafts striking the center ring, whereat loud and long cheers went up. Clifton and Kenneth were not so true. Both missed the target, each with a single shaft. Then came Little John's turn. He stepped forward to the line with his great seven-foot bow, and loosed his shafts so fast that it seemed to the beholders as if they had been sped with a single pull of the string.

All the arrows hung safe on his target. He knew another round must needs be shot, and he only wished to equal the rest. No cheering was heard, and all the people watched closely as Robin stepped forward with modest mien and held up his long-bow of greater length than his own body. He slowly pulled from his quiver his best shaft, one of those he had himself tied with feathers from the wild swan's wing.

He looked first at the King, and next at the Queen. Then,

ROBIN HOOD

with a faint smile, he sped his shaft to the very center of the
target. Resting his bow upright, he said: "Good Tepus, for
this round I rest upon that shot alone."

Still there was no cheering. The field was as if peopled with
marble statues. At last came whispering sounds, gradually
growing louder, till it was wafted on the faint wind to Robin's
ear that his shot was merely a stroke of luck and could not
be repeated.

"Master," whispered John, "shoot again to show that it was
no chance shot."

"Nay, nay, John, be patient. Let the archers go on in their
rightful turns."

With a slight paleness in his face, Tepus once more made a
trial, taking the most careful aim. Gilbert followed, and both
lodged their shafts in the center, making them even with Robin.
The people were now wild with delight, because their favorites,
though they had made no better shots than Robin, yet, having
two arrows in the center ring, would win the day unless Robin
should by a miracle do better.

The score now stood two center shots against one. Then Little
John once more took his bow, and this time shot with greater
care. But though he placed all his shafts very near the center,
he failed to beat the King's men. The King smiled, and bade
the Bishop of Hereford, who looked somewhat surly and downcast, be of good cheer.

Now Robin took off his bow-string and put on a new one without fray or flaw. Slowly and calmly he again took his place
at the line. In his seventy years of venturesome life he had
won many a match, and never had he been worsted with the
long-bow. He felt that his Queen placed great trust in his skill.
To say sooth, she had gone far toward quarreling with her husband, King Henry, whose temper was something of the shortest,
while his power made it unsafe for any to cross his will.

But of this Robin took no thought. To his simple mind,
he was there at the Queen's bidding, to do her honor, to win
the prize, and to maintain the fame of himself and his com-

ROBIN WINS THE QUEEN'S PRIZE

ROBIN HOOD

rades who loved him. He knew exactly what he could do. All was in his favor; the bright sun was behind him to give a white light on the target, and not a breath of air stirred to mar his aim. He alone of the vast throng was calm. He could easily have played with the people, and teased them as a cat does a mouse, by prolonging the contest.

At last he raised the bow, and, drawing the string to the utmost length of the shaft, held it there so long and so steadily that the people wondered if he were struck stiff, though in truth 'twas but a moment he stood so.

Twang! and the shaft sped, quick as light. The arrow split the wand in twain, and still in its flight pierced clean through the target in the very middle.

A burst of genuine delight rent the air, and even the King could not choose but cheer. The people stopped their shouts of a sudden, for they saw Robin nock another shaft and shoot once more. The second time, he split his own arrow that stood straight in the target's center. Again, for the third time, an arrow went whizzing, and the second shaft was split in twain.

Then Robin unstrung his great bow, and, hanging it over his back, he strode calmly down to make his obeisance to the Queen. Little John followed at his master's heels, and the King's archers came some distance behind.

Finsbury Field was a very bedlam. The crowd rushed up to the targets to view them close at hand and finger the broken shafts, for this was a thing that would be told to their children in song and story for many a year to come.

As Robin bent his knee, the King scowled darkly, and without a word he rose from his seat and left the pavilion.

Then Queen Eleanor said, smiling: "Rise, most gallant and brave archer! Thou hast won the prize—nay, much more, thou hast made for thyself in this our capital city an enduring name. Worthily hast thou done, and thy victory shall remain a bright and splendid deed of our reign. We will give command to send the prizes whithersoever thou wilt have them."

"Nay, fair and gracious Queen," quoth Robin, "Tepus and

ROBIN HOOD

Gilbert are good archers; upon them, I pray, bestow the prizes. I need no hart of Dalton Forest, nor wine, nor beer, for we have enough and to spare. But the silver bugle and gold-tipped arrow, an it please thee, give to myself and my good John, that we may ever keep them, in remembrance of this our visit."

"As thou dost desire, brave outlaw, so it shall be done. But this I must tell thee, bold Robin: I would fain be sure that thou wouldst instantly depart from this our city, that thou mayst come to thy home in the North without scathe. The King is deeply angered, and, though we may trust to his promise, some treacherous one, thinking to please him, may strive to do thee harm. So tarry not, but leave the city at once, under the guidance of my page, Richard Patrington."

"We will obey," quoth Robin. "But first I fain would speak a word with yon Bishop concerning our wager." Then, turning to where the Bishop of Hereford was seated, he said:

"Sir Bishop, thy wager is lost, but take it back as a recompense for that we took from thee in merry Sherwood."

"Nay, now, master," said Little John, under his breath, "that shall not be. We must divide it as a gift to the King's servants in return for their good service on Finsbury Field."

Quoth Robin: "Gracious Queen, honest Little John here hath put me in mind that we owe something in courtesy to the King's servants. Therefore, with thy good leave, we will fee them out of the Bishop's purse, sin he hath fairly lost this wager."

Then the Bishop's heart was as black as the glance he shot toward John, for he had hoped to gather in Robin's money along with his own.

When they had given largess of the money the Bishop had lost, they followed young Patrington, and were soon lost among the dense crowd, on their way back to their home in Sherwood Forest.

XXIII

ROBIN PURSUED BY THE KING

OUNG PATRINGTON guided the two archers toward the inn where their horses had been left in charge of Will Scarlet and Allan-a-Dale. They all mounted and rode together through Highgate, where they got upon Ermine Street, that led due north toward Hertford, Northampton, and Nottingham. When they were safe on the great highway, young Patrington left them and returned to the Court. The four outlaws were a merry party, riding abreast and chatting together of their doings in London town. Will Scarlet was disappointed at seeing so little of the city and its citizens, of which he had heard so much, but Robin saw the wisdom of their hasty retreat. So they trotted leisurely on, meaning to put up at St. Albans for the night.

Now when the King arose from his seat in such great anger he went to his chamber; and in due time the Queen followed, with divers officials and dignitaries of the Court. Hiding his vexed spirit from the Queen, the King asked for the Bishop, and when he had found him he took him aside.

"How now, Bishop?" quoth he. "Canst thou not devise some plan to ensnare these two outlaw villains and bring them

ROBIN HOOD

back hither? For I know that thou hast good cause to hate them."

"Yea, by the mass, that I have. These many years have I hoped to see the sly fox trapped, and it would be a goodly sight for me to behold the naughty thief dangling by the neck from some tall tree."

"Then," said the King, "let us together follow after, with a score of men-at-arms, to cut him off ere he reach his den."

"Ay," quoth the Bishop, "that would be merry—but the promise to the Queen."

"The Queen," replied Henry, "must not know. Therefore be ready early to-morrow, and I will give out that we go on a peaceful mission."

Now young Patrington, who had returned and was talking to his brother, one of the men-at-arms, chanced to learn of the plot, and straightway went to tell the Queen. Thereat her Majesty was sore vexed, and she bade young Richard ride hard and fast that night to overtake the little band of outlaws and warn them of their peril. So he mounted his horse and, galloping as fast as the wind, came at break of day to St. Albans, where he soon found Robin and his comrades making ready for an early start.

"What is the matter, my fair young page?" said Robin. "Doth the Queen again command our services?"

"Nay," replied the page, "but that dastard Bishop hath persuaded the King to follow you with men-at-arms and to hang you all upon a tree. The Queen bade me ride on before, to warn you; for they have by this time started, and will soon be upon you."

"Go back and carry our grateful thanks to our fair Queen, and say that we will guard us well." So young Richard departed, and rode on his way back to London town.

"Now, my comrades," quoth Robin, "we must here scatter, leave the highway, and take to the woods and by-paths. We will sell our horses and go afoot." But Little John would have none of this plan. Much better it seemed to him to ride apace and get

ROBIN HOOD

to Sherwood before the score of men-at-arms, that they might defend their trysting-place against them.

"Do as it pleaseth thee," quoth Robin, "for in this matter I will lay no command upon any. But for mine own part, I will go afoot."

So Little John, Will, and Allan galloped fast, and reached Sherwood safe and sound without let or hindrance. But Robin led his horse through the town seeking a buyer. Anon he met a milkman with a mule, upon whose back were slung two milk-cans. The milkman wore a long shepherd's smock, covering his body down to his shoes, and upon his head he had a squirrel-skin hood with a tail hanging down upon either side of his face. "Good faith," quoth merry Robin to himself, "this garb will suit me well."

"Good milkman," said he, "wilt thou change thy old rickety mule for my horse and trappings, and thy ragged smock - coat for my scarlet raiment, with ten bright shillings to boot?"

"Right blithely," quoth the milkman. Then, taking off his smock in a trice, for fear Robin should repent him of so unequal a bargain, he threw the smock in his face and laid hold upon the horse's bridle.

"Not so fast," quoth Robin. "Take my plumed cap for thy skin hood." The change was made, and both parted well content.

Robin jogged alongside his mule and milk-pails till about the hour of noon, when he stopped at a little village for food and rest. While he sat on a bench, quietly munching a piece of hard rye bread and now and then taking a draught of milk from a small cup that he found with the cans, what was his surprise to see a company of men-at-arms riding up with the King and the Bishop in the lead! They came at a sharp trot, yet one of the men turned aside, saying, "Milkman, hast thou seen four mounted archers pass along this road?"

Then Robin made answer: "Was one arrayed in scarlet, the others in green?"

"Yea, so they were."

ROBIN HOOD

"Then," said Robin, "go straight ahead, and ye will catch them soon."

Without more words the man galloped away to join the others, and all then mended their pace.

Now Robin knew full well that they would soon come back from this vain quest, so he gave his milk-cans to an old woman and cut him a stout cudgel from the wayside. Then, throwing his leg over the mule's back, he walloped the poor beast with might and main, and went bibity-bump along the main highway, hoping to reach Fountains Abbey in Needwood Forest before the dawn. So after journeying all night he came to the Abbey at break of day, thoroughly tired out, his back and arm full sore with belaboring the slothful mule.

Just as Robin had foreseen, the King and the Bishop soon retraced their steps. When they questioned other wayfarers they learned that no such men as those they sought had passed along that road, and they were full wroth that the milkman had befooled them. They found the milk-cans, and as soon as the old woman had told them the way that Robin had taken, they galloped off in full cry after their prey.

Meanwhile Robin, by good fortune, found Friar Cecil at Fountains Abbey. After partaking of a good meal, which the Friar soon set before him, he said:

"Now, good Cecil, I must tarry here no longer, for those hounds are in full cry, and the Bishop, who leads the King in quest of me, knoweth this place. Therefore, if they come before I go, the men-at-arms will surround the Abbey, and I am undone. Get me, then, pious Cecil, a palmer's habit, to don in place of this milkman's attire, which thou must bury in the garden. As for the mule, I will leave it in this place, for it is a dull beast that hindereth me and availeth not for speed."

Then Robin strode off, with his palmer's staff and bottle, at a swinging pace, that he might be well on his way before the King and his company should reach the Abbey. Three hours later the King and the Bishop stood knocking at the door, while the men-at-arms closed in around the little hermitage.

ROBIN HOOD

"By my mitered staff," roared the Bishop, "we've trapped the wily fox at last! For there stands the mule upon whose back he rode to this, his den."

"Open," shouted the King, "or we will dash the door to splinters."

Then Cecil unchained the door, holding a small book in his hand, and asked, with a pious, wondering look: "What can the matter be that ye do so rudely disturb my vesper devotions?"

"Reason enow!" quoth the Bishop. "Thy devotions must e'en wait till we have skimmed the cream from the milkman that lies hidden in some hole of thy den. Know, young Friar, that the Bishop of Hereford speaks! Therefore bring forth straightway the owner of the mule."

"I gladly give myself up, as owner of the mule, to thee, my Lord Bishop. Enter, then, good sirs. Search, rest, accept food and drink, and take whatever ye will."

The King and the Bishop went in and hurriedly searched the room, but found naught to show that any stranger had been there. "Hath no man come hither in the night?" asked the Bishop.

"None but a poor old palmer," replied Cecil, "who hath gone home on his way to Trentham Abbey."

Said the Bishop to the King, "In faith, the sly rogue hath changed his coat again."

When they had eaten and drunk and rested for an hour, they started on to Trentham, little the wiser for the many questions they asked of Friar Cecil. Robin was now a long way on his journey, and had reached the little town of Stafford. He was full sure that his pursuers would be thrown off the scent at Fountains Abbey, but in this he gave the Bishop too little credit for craft. You must know that Robin had an old acquaintance at the little Priory of Trentham in Friar Tunnicliffe, whom he had befriended in times gone by. He trusted that the friar would now give him a hearty welcome, and mayhap shelter him till the King's wrath abated.

It was the last thing in his mind to lead the King and the Bishop

ROBIN HOOD

to Sherwood; for, though he doubted not that in fair fight his yeomen could beat the King's sevenscore men-at-arms, yet he feared that, by ill luck, the King himself might be wounded or killed by an arrow. That would mean that an army would be sent against the outlaws. For this cause Robin sought to entice the King away from the forest.

Friar Tunnicliffe was a very pious and godly man, whose prayers were almost as long as his appetite. It was his boast that he could eat like a lion and sleep like a babe, yet he was wondrous thin and meager of face, so that he seemed ever as if he fasted. When Robin knocked at the Priory door he was admitted, like all pilgrims. Straightway he asked for Friar Tunnicliffe; and when he made himself known, the good friar fell upon his neck, bellowing and blubbering and bedewing him with tears of gladness. Robin then told of the sad plight he was in, and who it was that pursued him.

"Do the King and the Bishop know," asked the good friar, "that thou meanest to abide with us?"

"Nay, that I know not," said Robin. "All depends upon young Cecil, whether he will tell the truth, or by craft persuade them to take another road."

"Be that as it may, we must at once get thee another disguise. Then, should they come here, I will go with thee some distance. Both dressed alike in our friars' gowns, with book and beads, cowl and hood, none shall take note of us. By my faith," he cried, when Robin had changed his attire, "thou art a better friar than I, and of a more pious and holy mien."

Just then they heard the clatter of horses' hoofs growing louder and louder on the great Watling highway, which passed directly by the Priory. Then Robin knew that the Bishop and the King were again upon him. Good Friar Tunnicliffe hastily took up his staff, and both strode on their way up the road toward Chester away from the approaching horsemen. When they had gone a short space the friar bade his friend a tender farewell and retraced his steps back to the Priory, while Robin trudged along toward Chester.

PRIOR WILLIAM PROVIDES A FEAST FOR THE KING
AND THE BISHOP

ROBIN HOOD

Now the Prior of Trentham was a jolly, fat, hospitable church-man, and there was always good eating and drinking to be had in his house. He was unaware of the meeting of Robin and the friar. When the Bishop and the King made known to him who they were and what was their purpose, he swelled with pride, for he liked nothing better than to feast a great man at his plenteous board; and now that he had the King with him, he vowed to give him a feast he would never forget. The King confessed he was growing weary of chasing this wily outlaw, and the Bishop's mouth always watered at mention of a feast.

As for Robin, he pushed along at a swinging pace, and was soon past the nunnery at Stoke. Up Hartshill and down along Thistlebery he went, on the way to Nantwich, where he stopped for a little to rest, but soon pressed on and reached Chester on the following noon. The King was sore weary after his hard ride of a hundred and fifty miles, and was well content to lie stretched at full length upon a downy couch in Prior William's chamber. Soon he became aware that the Priory had a larder well stored with good things, for a pleasing odor was wafted to his nostrils on the gentle morning breeze.

Prior William of Trentham both knew how to provide all sorts of dainties and rich dishes and was himself a gallant trencher-man. It was his wont to stuff himself till unbidden tears trickled down his ruddy cheeks at the sad thought that no more could be tucked away. Then he would sleep away his heaviness, snoring loudly. Throughout the feast he scarce spake, save ever and anon to bid his guests be merry and make good cheer.

"Truly," quoth the King, at last, "I am full sore, so well have I fared. And thy rich, brown ale hath a nutty flavor that maketh me ever crave it the more."

"I am honored," quoth the jolly Prior, "that my King doth commend my simple fare. The ale is of a special brew, of the finest Kentish hops and Staffordshire barley, with the pure waters of our silvery Trent—of which, by the mass, my cellar shall never run dry, though my own need requires four gallons each day, and two extra of Sundays and saints' days."

[269]

ROBIN HOOD

"Methinks," said the King, slyly, "saints' days come nigh
every day in the year."

"Marry, that they do," quoth the Prior, "and I make my
vow never to miss one."

The King and the Bishop were now fully satisfied and ready for
rest, so they laid them down, and were soon slumbering, forgetful
of the chase. Meanwhile brave Robin was carrying a message
from Friar Tunnicliffe to a brother at St. Dunstan's Abbey,
which set forth that he was a poor monk on his way to London
and that any aid given him would benefit the Church. For he
had made up his mind that his safest course would be to go back
to London, where through the Queen's good help he might
win the King's pardon.

The good friar of St. Dunstan's received him with much
kindness, telling him that some holy fathers were going to London on the morrow, and that he would furnish him with a mount.

"Much thanks," quoth Robin, "and take these five pounds
for the poor of the parish as a gift in return for thy help." So
he set forth in company with the priests, and when he arrived
in London he left them and hied to Court.

When he came before Queen Eleanor, he fell down upon his
knee before her and said, "An it please thee, gracious Queen, I
am come to speak with King Henry."

Queen Eleanor answered bold Robin, "The King is gone to
merry Sherwood, and when he went he said, 'I go to seek Robin
Hood.' "

"Then fare thee well, my Queen. To Sherwood I will hie
apace, for I fain would see what it is that the King would have,
if I can but meet with his Majesty."

But when King Henry came home, he had not yet set eyes
upon Robin Hood.

"Thou art welcome home, Henry, my sovereign liege," said
the Queen. "That bold archer, Robin Hood, hath been here
to seek thy person."

When the King heard that Robin had been to Court seeking
him, he laughed and answered: "He is a cunning knave, for we

ROBIN HOOD

have sought him this whole three weeks, uphill and down dale, through town and village, through woodland and field, yet the crafty fox escaped us."

"A boon, a boon!" cried Queen Eleanor. "I beg it here of your grace, to pardon his life and seek no more to take him."

"By my crown and scepter, he shall have pardon. So brave and bold a heart I like well. So crafty and wise an outlaw doth deserve the freedom of his merry woodland life. If the Bishop will have Robin Hood, let him go a-hunting alone, for I have had enough."

XXIV

ROBIN RESCUES THE WIDOW'S SONS

OBIN kept his word to the Queen that he would hie apace back to Sherwood, and never before in all his life did he enter the oak glade more glad at heart. Though Little John and his comrades had feared no whit for his safety, yet they gave him a mighty cheer when at last they saw him come forth from the forest trees. So, when they had feasted well, they sat them down to talk, for it was early evening.

"How sweet to my ear," quoth Robin, "is the song of that throstle, pouring out thanks to God! And so, too, do I thank my Maker, that I am here once more safe and sound among my own dear comrades, after such a chase as the King gave me. As for that fat Bishop, I make a vow, when next we have him here, to make him fast forty days and nights. I'll warrant I will square his roundness."

The Bishop never again came nigh Sherwood Forest, and for some weeks all went quietly in the glade. But it fell upon a merry May day that Robin Hood set forth for Nottingham, and by the wayside he spied an old woman sitting, who rocked to and fro and wept full sore.

"COME, CHANGE THINE APPAREL FOR MINE, OLD MAN"

ROBIN HOOD

"What is the matter, good woman," he asked, "that thou dost so weep and mourn?"

"The matter is bad enough, good sir," quoth she. "In Nottingham town this day three of my sons must die, and thou seest me a poor widow left alone to pine."

"What have they done?" said Robin Hood. "Have they slain priest or friar, or have they burned the farmers' hayricks?"

"Nay, good sir, none of these things have they done."

"Then what have they done, I pray thee tell unto me?"

" 'Tis for slaying of the King's fallow deer," said she. "Though they did bear their long-bows in thy company, they were ambushed and taken by the Sheriff's men, and are now lost to me for ever."

"Say not so, good woman, by the truth of my body," quoth bold Robin Hood. "Thou hast told me in good time, and be assured thy sons shall come safe to thee again."

"Art thou not Robin Hood?" quoth the old woman.

"In very truth, that I am. Dost thou not remember how thou didst make me dine and sup with thee in thy cottage when I was in danger? Now, therefore, I will gather my men, and we will save thy sons to thee." Then he gave three loud blasts upon his horn, and all his men came running over the lea.

"My comrades," said Robin, "three of our men are this day condemned to die. Therefore, I pray you, go back and cover your green coats with mantles, then meet me at the hangman's tree."

He himself strode away to Nottingham town, and when he drew nigh the gate he met an old palmer walking slowly along the highway.

"What news, good palmer?" he cried. "What news of the town this fair day?"

The old man answered, "Three squires in Nottingham town are to die this day for slaying of the King's deer."

"Come, change thine apparel for mine, old man," quoth Robin. "Here are forty shillings in good silver, go spend it in food and drink."

"Alack-a-day, ne'er laugh an old man to scorn, wherever

ROBIN HOOD

thou goest; for my apparel is torn and ragged, and thine is rich and good."

"What is that to thee, thou silly old man? I have need of thy ragged old clothes, and here are twenty pieces of good gold that I will give for them."

The palmer, with wondering eyes, took the money; and Robin put on the old man's hat, which stood full high in the crown. Then he cast over his shoulder the cloak, patched with black and blue and red. Next he put on the old man's breeches, which were also patched all over. "By the truth of my body, when I am fully dressed," quoth Robin, "I can truly say, 'This man loved little price.'" Then he put on the palmer's shoes, that were patched beneath and full of holes above. Robin looked himself over with a wry smile, then, bidding the palmer God-speed, he walked on to the town. There, wandering up and down the streets, he chanced to meet the proud Sheriff.

"The saints save thee, dread Sheriff," quoth he. "What wilt thou give to a silly old man to-day to be hangman?"

Now the Sheriff had been hunting all over the town, yet had found no one who would do the deed, so this offer was just to his liking. "The hangman's fee to-day," he replied, "is thirteen pence and the three suits of the men that are to die upon the gallows." Then Robin twirled around and gave a lively hop, skip, and jump. "Nay, by the mass," quoth the Sheriff, "that is a lively caper for an old man."

"I was ne'er a hangman in all my life," cried Robin, "nor do I like the trade, for a curse is upon the man that was first a hangman. Proud Sheriff, I have a horn in my pocket, that I got from Robin Hood, and a blast from it would blow thee little good."

"Oh, wind that horn, thou ragged fellow," said the Sheriff. "I care not though thou blow such a blast that both thine eyes fall out."

Then Robin took the horn from under his ragged coat and blew both loud and shrill. Instantly a hundred and fifty of his men were seen running up the street.

ROBIN HOOD

"Who are those men," the Sheriff said, "that run so hard and fast?"

Brave Robin replied, "In truth, they are friends of mine, come to pay a visit to thee." Straightway he took a sword from one of his men and led the band on to the prison door, while a dozen stout yeomen took the Sheriff and bound him hand and foot. When the prison guards saw Robin and Little John, they fell on their knees begging for mercy and gave up the key of the prison. Soon the three young men were given their freedom.

"Now come with me, my three brave fellows," quoth Robin. "I wish to bring you back myself to your weeping mother." So Robin led the three brothers to the widow's cottage, and when they all stood before her, he said, "Good widow, as I promised, I have freed thy three sons and now bring them back to thee safe and sound."

"The saints shower blessings upon thy head, bold Robin Hood, and a widow's prayer follow thee where'er thou dost go."

Now while Robin was doing this good deed, a sad thing befell without his knowledge. Some of his men took up the gallows and placed it, as well as the Sheriff, upon a cart; then, with a mighty shout, they dragged it to an open glade in the forest. The Sheriff now saw that his last hour was nigh. He knew that these men were grimly resolved to revenge themselves for his cruelty through many long years. His own men had forsaken him, and he thought it hard they should leave him to die the most ignoble death known to man, yet he bethought him that this death was but the same he had planned for three of their own band at this very hour. His mind went back to Will Stutely and to Little John—how near they had been to a like fate. He quaked to see how fast they worked to set up the gallows. In but a few more moments he, old in the service of the King, was to breathe his last. Then four brawny fellows laid their heavy hands on him and bound his arms tightly to his body with hide thongs.

"Where, oh, where is Robin, your captain, and where is Little

John?" moaned the Sheriff, in piteous tones. "They would never see done so foul a deed, for with all their faults I have never known them to stain their fame with cold-blooded murder."

"No, thou wretch," said one outlaw, "but we know what thou wouldst have done, this very hour, and many a time before. Didst thou e'er have mercy upon us? Think on Will Stutely— saved from the very gallows, and these to-day, our comrades, three brothers, worthy sons of a poor lone widow! Three good men for shooting a deer! Away with him—hanging's too good for such a knave!"

Thus died the Sheriff of Nottingham, not with the will or knowledge of Robin Hood, but through the hasty anger of some of his men who had grown lawless in his old age.

'Twas but an hour later when Robin, Little John, and Will Stutely were returning to the oak glade, happy indeed that they had given back to the poor old widow her three young sons. As they turned from a little fern-clad path into an open glade they saw hanging high above them the body of a man hung up by the neck.

"God-a-mercy!" quoth Robin, "what have we here? And who are they that would defile our woods with such a horrid sight?"

But Will Stutely at once understood what had been done. "Our men," quoth he, "have done here the worst day's work of their lives, dear uncle. That is the Sheriff of Nottingham that hangs so high in air."

"What!" shouted Robin and Little John in the same breath. "Nay, nay, our men would not of their own free will be guilty of so foul a deed." Then Robin put his horn to his mouth and blew three loud blasts, and then another three. Ere the echoes died away the whole band came running at full speed through the forest and ranged themselves before him.

"My loved and brave companions of many years," said Robin Hood, gazing up at the grim-looking thing aloft, "is this the work of mine own band?"

None gave answer, and none dared look their leader in the face, but all hung their heads in shame.

ROBIN HOOD

" 'Tis a black day's work that ye have done for us all, and by it we shall all pay dearly but justly. What can we do, think ye, my men? We cannot leave the grim thing hanging there. Who is there among you that dares take the body back to Nottingham? The townsfolk know full well ye took the Sheriff away along with the gallows. In a little while the King will be told, and then what think ye he will do?" With bowed heads Robin and Little John left the place, and the men silently followed on at a distance behind.

Five days had passed since the Sheriff met his fate. The outlaws went about their usual affairs in glum silence. The merry song and laughter had died away; the glade was silent and gloomy. Robin and John felt a storm was brewing, so they got together a fair share of their treasure and money and brought it to Fountains Abbey. On the sixth day one of the widow's sons came and stood before Robin Hood.

"What news," quoth Robin, "hast thou to give a broken old man?"

"Dire and black is the news, bold Robin. The Sheriff's men have cut down the body, and all the town and country is ablaze with rage. Yet they know that neither Little John nor thou had part in the crime. The King hath sent five companies of archers, with knights and men-at-arms, all to storm the oak glade and kill every outlaw. My two brothers have been seized, and on pain of death must guide the army to this place on the morrow soon after break of day. I alone have ventured to tell the tale and warn thee."

Then Robin called his men around him, and told them what was in store for them. "Go, my comrades all," he said, "to the treasury, and share among yourselves whatever may be therein. Take all ye want from the armory, the clothiery, and the buttery. But see that ye share alike. Take the goods to whatever hiding-places ye like, but let them be far from here. Henceforth each man must be his own master. Go where ye will, but stay not here to see another sunrise. For myself, I

[279]

ROBIN HOOD

will hie to Fountains Abbey, there to await my end and patiently endure what judgment the King may lay upon me. If I should be pardoned, then with the help of young Friar Cecil I will give myself to God and our good Lady dear, till the final day."

At these last words he turned aside; and many of the outlaws wept scalding tears as they slowly moved away for the final sharing of their goods, of which there was enough to place them all above want for many years to come. In such wise did Robin leave them, well-nigh heartbroken with sorrow and shame. Followed by Little John and Cecil, he strode from the glade into the leafy forest; and with one glance backward he saw, through his blinding tears, the last of his woodland home of the merry, happy past.

As the sun set, like a blood-red ball flickering through the leafy trees behind the great oak, the glen was lonely and silent. Not a single footfall touched the greensward that for threescore years and more had been trampled by many feet. At morning, at noon, and at evening, the air had resounded with music, song, and merry jest, with laughter and jocund jollity. But now all was changed and still. The sevenscore archers, in large and small groups, had gone their ways. The birds now sang to themselves a doleful ditty; their merry human companions had left them never to return.

Early on the following morn, archers and men-at-arms could be seen tearing down the two great towers. The great oak, with its secret passage, was cut to pieces; the beautiful bower that Robin had kept fresh and green since the day, years agone, when Marian had died, was leveled to the ground. Indeed, all that the outlaws had made for their use and comfort was clean destroyed. Such was the doleful and bitter end of Robin Hood's woodland home in Sherwood Forest.

XXV

ROBIN HOOD'S DEATH AND BURIAL

**A**ND now, with sad, aching hearts, we go to Fountains Abbey, lovingly and piously built, stone upon stone, by the jolly Friar Tuck, whose body rests peacefully beside the trickling fountain. In the little, well-known cell we find the bold and brave Robin Hood. What a change has come over the dear, kindly face in a few hours! His hair and beard seem to have grown quite white in a single day. His strong, sturdy body, of late so youthful, now looks loose and limp. His cheerful, manly voice has become low and sad-toned. Young Cecil begs him to take some barley-broth and then lie down in sleep to forget his woe.

"Nay, nay, my gentle Cecil," quoth Robin, "I have no wish to eat or drink; and as for sleep, I am not worthy of such a boon."

"Alack, good master," said Little John, with a rising lump in his throat, "take it not so to heart. Thou art not to blame, or the King would have been here ere now, for he knoweth thy retreat."

Quoth Robin: "I am not able to shoot one shot more, and my arrows will not again flee. Take me, then, sweet Little John, to Kirkley nunnery, that my cousin—who is the abbess and well

ROBIN HOOD

skilled in leechcraft—may bleed me and so heal me of my illness. Help me, pious Cecil, to fair Kirkley, that the abbess may mend my state." So they placed him upon a litter drawn by a mule, and with Little John and tall, young Cecil walking on either side, he came by easy stages to the nunnery. Little John rang the bell to call the abbess.

"Come in," quoth she, when she saw Robin, "and drink some wine to strengthen thy body."

"Nay, my cousin, I will neither eat nor drink till thou hast bled me."

"Well, Cousin Robin, I have a room in the tall tower which thou hast never seen; and if it please thee to enter, I will do that which thou dost desire."

When Little John and Cecil would have followed after, the abbess said: "Go back, go back, our skill is sufficient and we need no help." So they stayed outside the nunnery and sat under the shade of a leafy tree, waiting, very down-hearted, till they should hear news of their master.

Now I must tell you that this wicked woman knew full well what had befallen the Sheriff of Nottingham, and in her evil heart she conceived it would please the King to hear of Robin's death. Thus she resolved so to bleed Robin that he would never recover. Taking him by the hand, she led him to a private room in the nunnery tower and tied his arm tight round with linen bands. Then she took a long sharp knife, and with evil intent cut into one of the larger veins, so that he would bleed fast and soon die. After she had done this she heartlessly left him alone in the room, locked the door, and went away out of sight and sound.

Robin soon grew weaker, and he cried aloud, begging for help; but no help was nigh. Then he got up and tried to raise the casement window, that he might leap down or cry out to his faithful John, but his weakness was so great that he could move it only a little. At last, weary and faint, he bethought him of his horn, which so oft had saved him from danger. Setting it to his lips, he blew three weak blasts.

[282]

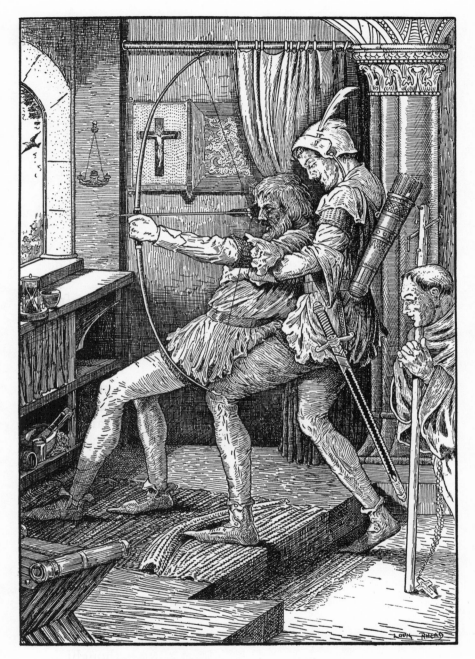

ROBIN SHOOTS HIS LAST SHAFT

ROBIN HOOD

When Little John heard the sound he leaped to his feet, crying: "I fear my master is near dead; he blows so wearily." Then he ran as fast as he could go to the nunnery door, but they would not open to him.

Nearly beside himself with rage, he looked about him and saw a massive piece of oak. Straightway he picked it up in his brawny arms and hurled it with such force that it split the strong door apart. Then, followed by Cecil, he ran up, screaming loudly, "Master, my dear master, I have come to save thee."

As he paused to listen he thought he heard a faint cry of distress; and, bounding up the steps of the tower, he threw his great body with a terrific bang against the door so that the lock burst. He found his poor master still bleeding and faint upon the floor.

"A boon, a boon, master," he cried, as he knelt and supported him in his arms.

"What is the boon," faintly asked Robin Hood, "that thou dost beg of me?"

"It is to burn this fair Kirkley Hall," quoth John, "and all their nunnery."

"Now, nay," quoth Robin Hood, "that boon I will not grant. I never hurt woman in all my life, nor man in woman's company, and now at the end of my life it shall not be. It is for God and our good Lady to wipe away all stains. Let these poor women be, for I am dying, dear John, and fain would be at peace with all now, as I wished when in health. Thou hast been ever a faithful comrade and dear brother, so let my end be without strife or guile. Now give me my long-bow in my hand, that through this window I may shoot one more shaft, and wheresoever it is taken up, there let my grave be dug."

Then the great, large-hearted John, with hot tears on his cheeks, lifted up his beloved master and carried him, tenderly as a mother carries her babe, to the open casement. Young Friar Cecil lifted up the great bow, nocked a shaft, and placed it in the weak, pale hands. Robin pulled the string as far as he could, and with a loud twang the shaft sped on its way.

ROBIN HOOD

"Oh, sweet music of my bow that lulls me to everlasting sleep!" quoth he. "A last boon, my faithful brothers, do I ask before I die. Lay a green sod before my head, and another at my feet, and place my bent bow by my side, that I may still hear its sweet music. Make the top of my grave of gravel and green shrubs. Let me have length and breadth enough to lie at ease. Then place a stone upon the sod, that they may say when I am dead, 'Here lies the bold Robin Hood.'"

Both readily promised him it should be done. Then gently and slowly his head fell upon John's breast, and his spirit winged its way. John carried his master tenderly down the winding stairs out of the nunnery, and they buried him where the arrow had struck beneath a wide-branching oak-tree.

So here we take leave of the noble and brave Robin Hood.

Little John and Friar Cecil went back to Fountains Abbey, but not to stay. Old memories were so closely woven about this little hermitage that they could not bear a life of loneliness there. So each one wended his own way. John went to join some relatives who lived at a little village called Hathersage in Derbyshire, where he lived a retired life for a few years, and where he was buried. Young Friar Cecil, with a long life-work before him, entered a priory, and gave himself wholly to the Church.

THE END

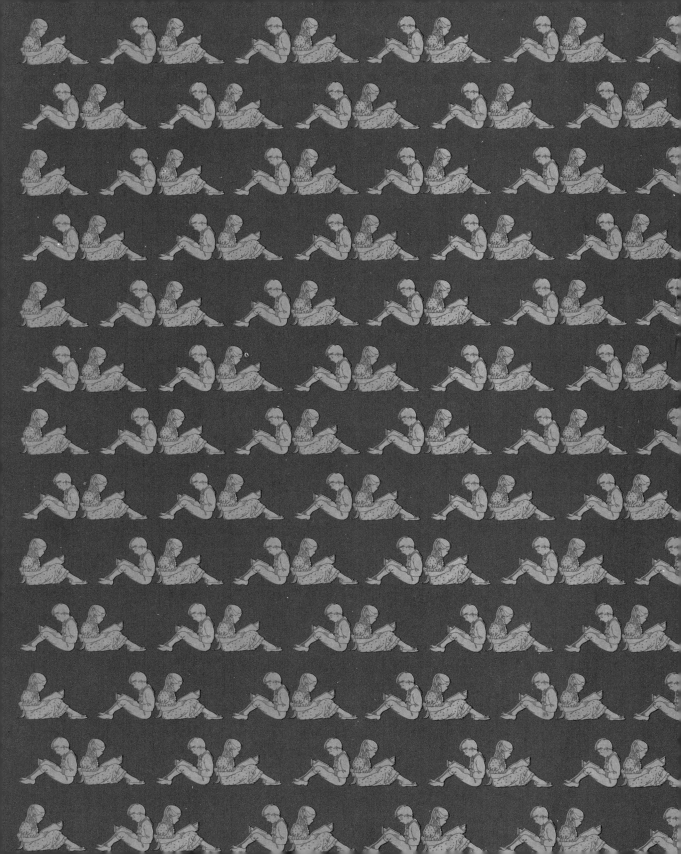